The Rings Book

The Rings Book

JINKS McGRATH

Krause Publications

To Granti and her inspirational longevity

First published in Great Britain 2002
A & C Black Publishers Ltd
37 Soho Square, London W1D 3QZ
www.acblack.com

Copyright © 2002 Jinks McGrath
info@jinksmcgrath.com

ISBN 0-7136-5393-0

Published simultaneously in the USA by Krause
Publications, Iola, Wis.

ISBN 0-87349-543-8

Library of Congress Catalog No: 2002105110

Front cover illustration: enamelled rings by
Jinks McGrath
Back cover illustration: anticlastic ring with black
onyx setting by Jinks McGrath
Frontispiece: the author's studio, photo by
Jinks McGrath

Cover design by Dorothy Moir
Design by Keith & Clair Watson

Printed and bound in Malaysia by Tien Wah Press

A&C Black uses paper produced with elemental
chlorine-free pulp, harvested from managed
sustainable forests

Note: jewelry making can sometimes involve the use
of sharp tools and dangerous substances. Please keep
items clearly labelled and out of the reach of children.
Neither the author nor publisher can accept any legal
liability for errors or ommissions

CONTENTS

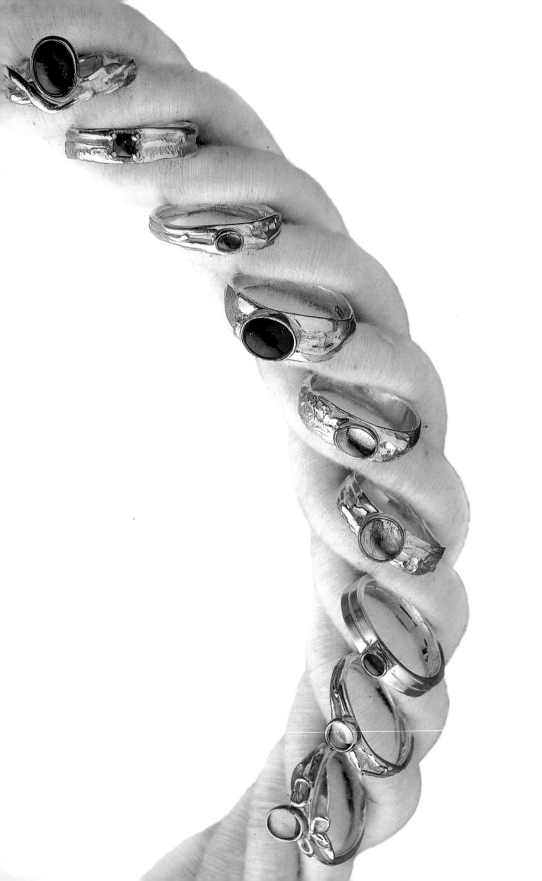

ACKNOWLEDGEMENTS

My first very big thank you is to photographer Paul Forrester, for the week he spent in my workshop setting up, taking, developing and providing me with all the pictures for this book. His patience and humour was much appreciated.

My second one is to Tony Tigg for the day spent here at the bench, astounding us all with his speed and skill, setting all the stones for Chapter 3, and at the same time providing me with an unexpected master class!

Thanks also to Jayanti, Hansa and Jo at Prabhu Enterprises for their generous loan of stones and taking such care with my detailed lists.

My particular and grateful thanks to everyone who sent me pictures of their work which makes up the gallery at the end of the book.

Stack of rings, by Mark Nuell.

INTRODUCTION

The ring. A token of love, affection and eternity. A very small thing, which speaks volumes about our continuing and probably subconscious need for symbols and yet, I believe, very much taken for granted. Although much of the formality associated with engagements and weddings is disappearing from Western cultures, couples contrive to give each other rings to symbolise their union. I wonder how aware we are of the cultural and religious significance the ring still portrays in our increasingly secular society?

In both the religious and civil act of marriage, one or sometimes two rings are given. An engagement is usually celebrated by the giving of a decorative ring, which gives out a clear but unspoken message when worn. Eternity rings are given to demonstrate continuing love, and messages spelt out in 'Regard' and 'Dearest' rings assure the wearer of the affection held for them by the giver.

Many women these days like to own a ring which complements a particular item of clothing or which demonstrate some sort of identity. When I am asked to design a ring, I like to find out as much as possible about significant events, particular colour preferences, what, if anything, is being celebrated, birth signs and seasons and anything else which may be relevant to the client before starting the design, so that I can try to marry-in subtle references to some or all of them.

Men too are increasingly happy to wear rings, although these still tend to be wedding and signet rings. However, I now find that they are much more interested in the design of their ring and often like to have something which also reflects an aspect of themselves as well as complementing their partner's ring. Thus the ring becomes a truly individual thing and although some of its history may be lost on future generations, it is likely to remain in the family for many years.

In my work I see many rings that have been passed down through generations. They provide one of the most personal links with our family history, and I'm sure could tell us all wonderful stories. . .

These tangible links are often hidden away in jewellery boxes and when found, bring back strong memories of the one who owned and wore the ring. As these rings, which were made and worn many years ago, do not always suit the fashion and style of the 21st century, the temptation to have them remodelled is very strong. I have to admit that one of my least favourite jobs as a jeweller is to remove stones from an old ring to reset them in a new one. It seems that the short-term satisfaction gained is a loss in the long term.

The gallery at the end of this book will go some way to justify my reluctance. Here we have some wonderfully imaginative, extra-ordinary work, all reflecting the jewellers' appreciation of life in the 21st century, fantastic use of the materials and thoughtful technology. These pieces will surely be heirlooms for our grandchildren and great grandchildren if they can make it through without being 'altered to suit' on the way. They will tell us as much about the world today as our grandmothers' rings tell us about the world of yesterday.

As a result of these thoughts, in this book I have put emphasis on forming the basic structures, which make up different types of rings, not necessarily the traditional ones. I have kept the structures relatively simple but all of them can be used as a base upon which to build something more exotic. Most of the rings in the gallery are built on one or other of the principle structures, which have then been taken further in a very personal way.

In the first chapter of the book we look at the structural form of the ring, beginning with a very simple band and then progressing to show how different patterns and formulae are used for getting height, shape and thickness onto that simple band. I have assumed a knowledge of some soldering and jewellery making techniques in this book. For those

From design to completion. Courtesy Jeanne Werge-Hartley

wishing for fuller explanations about the techniques, I would suggest further reading; *The Encyclopaedia of Jewellery Making Techniques* by Jinks McGrath and other books such as *Jewellery – Fundamentals of Metalsmithing* by Tim McCreight.

The second chapter looks at making and attaching the means of decorating the ring, whether it is for a stone or enamel or simply mixing metals. Most of the principles will also be relevant to other ideas.

In the third chapter, with the much appreciated assistance of the master setter Tony Tigg, I have looked at the principles of fixing the stones or decorations in their place. Again, some of these techniques could apply to mediums other than stones, but the principles remain the same.

I have included a chart about stones as it seemed an appropriate addition in a book about rings. The longer I have been making jewellery the more I find myself drawn to the magic of stones, be they precious, semi-precious or just something fascinating which has been found on a beach or whilst out walking in the hills. There are so many myths, stories and meanings attached to stones which we can all relate to our own circumstances and that give reason and individuality when choosing which stones to use.

The fourth chapter is concerned with finishing. There are many ways of achieving different looks and textures, some of which are explained here – from a highly polished finish to a more contemporary matt finish.

As you will see, I have not even tried to demonstrate making anything very individual or imaginative. This is a book concerned with looking at the principles and basic necessities for ring making, which I hope will provide a foundation to which can be added your own imagination and creativity.

Ring by Elizabeth Olver.

CHAPTER ONE

Building Shanks

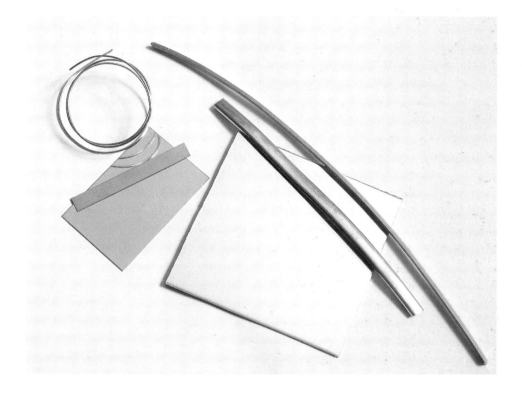

This chapter is devoted to building up the shapes to make different types of rings. Some rings require formulae and patterns to work out the shape whilst others build up from a simple band. The following rings show how the various shapes are made and from these you will be able to build up ideas for more intricate designs. Making the mounts, collets and bezels for rings with stones is covered in chapter 2, and setting the stones is described in chapter 3.

Before beginning to make a ring, we must have an idea of the metal we want to make it with, how wide we want the band to be, how thick we want the metal to be and whether it is to be a plain band or have some decoration.

In this first chapter we start right at the beginning by making a simple band.

1. Plain Band Ring

1. Cut a length of binding wire and loop it around the ring stick or mandrel at the marked position. Tighten up the ends by twisting them with a pair of flat-nosed pliers until the wire is tight.

MATERIALS
Silver sheet 0.8mm thick.
Hard silver solder.

Finding the length of silver required for the ring

This method can be used to measure the length of almost any ring. First the finger is measured using a set of ring sizers – these are calibrated with letters A–Z and some have $^1/_2$ measurements in between. The correct letter size is placed onto a 'ring stick' or mandrel, and a note is made where it fits exactly. On a 'ring stick' this should be marked with a similar letter and on a mandrel you will need to make a little mark with marker ink.

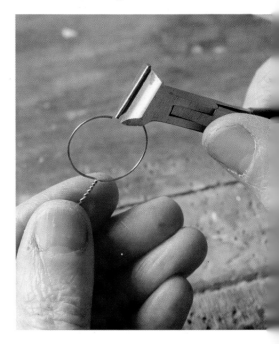

2. Remove the wire from the mandrel and cut the circle open opposite the twisted ends.

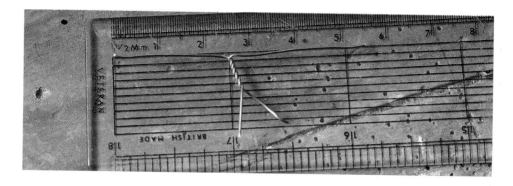

3. Straighten out the wire so that it becomes a straight line. This is the length you will require for the inside of your ring.

As the silver has a thickness to it, the outside measurement of the ring will be slightly larger than the inside. To allow for this difference, add approximately twice the thickness of the silver, i.e. add 1.6mm onto the length established by the binding wire as the thickness of the silver being used for this ring is 0.8mm. Mark the length of the binding wire plus the 1.6mm on the silver sheet.

In practice I would rather round the measurement up slightly which allows the ends of the metal to be filed straight if necessary.

4. Having decided on the width of the ring, in this case it is 8mm, open out a pair of dividers to 8mm. Place one side against the side of the silver and the other side on the silver. Run down the side of the silver with the dividers, thus drawing a parallel line on the surface of the silver.

Making the plain band ring

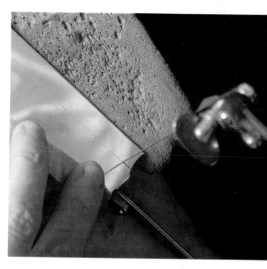

5. Use a piercing saw to cut out along the scribed line.

As this piece of silver is only 0.8mm thick it will not be necessary to anneal it. However, if you are using

15

anything thicker than 1mm it should
be annealed first and then pickled.

8. File away any excess solder from all
around the join.

6. Use half-round pliers (with the
curved side on the inside of the ring)
to bend the ring ends round so that
they sit closely together.
If you can make them sit tight up to
each other and in a straight line at
this stage, you will find that the
soldering will be much easier.

9. The ring is now shaped on the
steel mandrel with a wooden mallet
until it is nicely rounded.

10. It is now ready to be finished.
File marks should be removed with
either a fine needle file or 240 wet
and dry paper.
Use finer grades of the wet and dry
until the surface of the silver is ready
to be polished on the wheel.
For information on 'finishing' see
Chapter 4.

7. Flux through and around the join
and use hard solder to solder up.
Quench and pickle. Rinse the piece in
water and dry it carefully.

2. Using D section wire

D section ring with cabochon garnet.

This little ring is simple to make and has a cabochon stone set in either copper or gold to make a contrasting effect with the silver. I used a garnet and 9 carat gold. As this chapter is just about making the shank and soldering on the piece for the stone, more information about making the collet can be found on page 71.

MATERIALS

4mm x 1.5mm silver D section wire approximately 6cm long.
Strip of either copper or gold for the setting.
Silver sheet, approximately 1.3mm thick, 10 x 10mm.
Cabochon stone, the one shown is a garnet 6.5 x 6.5mm.
Hard and easy silver solder.

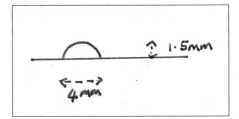

When working out the length of D section needed for a ring, you will need to measure the height of the 'D'.

In this case the D section used was 1.5mm high, so I added 3mm onto the total length of wire.

I usually make the collet for the stone first. You will find this explained on page 71.

After you have made the collet, place it onto the silver sheet (which should not yet be cut to size) ready for soldering.

The reason for leaving the sheet bigger than you need at this stage is

17

because it is more difficult to solder the collet absolutely centrally onto the finished base than it is to cut out the base accurately after the collet has been soldered on.

Solder the collet to the silver with hard solder. If you are using gold for the collet take care not to overheat when soldering. The silver solder can eat into the gold leaving quite deep pot marks on the outer surface.

At worst, a low carat gold can start to disappear into the silver!

After pickling and rinsing, use a pair of dividers to mark a line outside the collet where the silver is to be cut away. Put one end of them against the inside of the collet and the other at the required distance away from it, on the silver. Draw them round the complete edge of the collet, marking the outside as you do so.

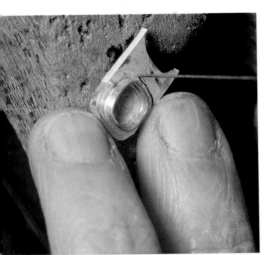

1. Pierce around the line you have marked and then clean up the edges with a flat needle file.

2. They can be slightly rounded for a softer effect.

3. Make the ring from the D section wire: use hard solder to join it. Use a flat file to make a flat area on top of the ring for the base of the setting to sit on.

Check that you are filing it flat by

turning it upside down and making sure it stands straight on a flat surface.

4. Hold the ring and the setting together with binding wire.

5. Place the ring upside down on the soldering block. I like to support the shank with a little piece of charcoal so that it does not move, and soldering this way up allows you to make sure that the ring is aligned properly with the top piece. Flux carefully along both sides where the ring meets the top. Use easy solder to solder the two together.

TIP When tightening binding wire, use flat-nosed pliers and twist the wire as near to the piece as possible. Tighten up gently until the pieces are firmly together and snip off any long bits of wire.

The ring is now ready to file and finish. For instructions on setting the stone, go to chapter 3, setting 1(a) on page 89.

TIP Cutting solder paillons is easier if you make one end of your solder thinner by either rolling it through the rolling mill or by hammering it thinner. Use snips to cut up the thinner end into four or five strips, and then use your top cutters to cut across the strips to make the paillons.

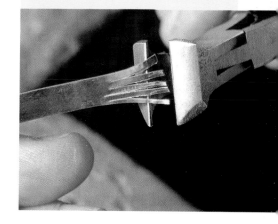

3. Double-banded Ring

Double-banded ring set with moonstone.

This ring can be used in many forms. In the ring shown, the top and bottom bands are made with D section wire and soldered on to the already made up ring. Square section wire could be used in place of D section. There is also scope for using contrasting metals.

MATERIALS

2.5mm x 1mm D section silver wire, approximately 15cm long.
Silver sheet either 0.8 or 1mm thick.
Metal for the collet (I used 18 carat gold).
Cabochon moonstone.

If you are setting a stone, as shown, onto this ring, make the collet first (see chapter 2, mount 2, page 72).

From the silver sheet, pierce out the length needed for your ring. Allow extra width at this stage, so that when the top and bottom bands are fitted, the edges of the ring protrude above them, which makes it easier to place the solder and easier to know that there is a good fit all the way round.

Make up the ring as described on page 14. After rounding it up on the mandrel, file the join and finish the outside carefully with the wet and dry papers until it is really clean. Do not neaten the top and bottom edges yet.

The reason for using round wire and then flattening it is because round wire is easier to bend initially but there needs to be a flat surface to solder onto the ring. If you solder round wire onto a ring there is always a visible line around the top and bottom edges. The wire is then soldered onto the metal to be used for the ring while it is still flat.

The metal on the outside of the wires is cut away before bending the ring up for soldering.

Now place some binding wire around the outside of the ring and twist to tighten, as you would when getting the measurement for a ring on the ring stick. Cut the wire and open it out straight. This gives you the inside measurement of the D section wire bands. For the actual length, you will need to add on approximately twice the height of the D.

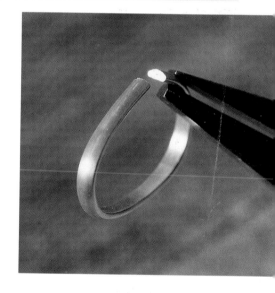

1. Make two rings from the D section, using hard solder.

If the D section rings distort slightly when they are being rounded up on the mandrel, lay them onto a flat steel surface and cover them with another piece of flat steel.

21

Hold the top steel parallel with the base and hit it directly with a flat hammer. This will straighten them.

Push the two D section rings onto the main ring. They should fit really snugly. If they are too big cut out a little section and resolder. If they are a little small, they can be stretched by placing them on the mandrel and hammering them down it with a wooden mallet. Anneal, if necessary, to assist the rings to stretch.

Once the two rings are pushed onto the main ring, make sure they are parallel with each other and there is enough room between them for the collet to be soldered on.

3. Solder the two outer rings to the inner one.

4. After pickling and rinsing, file away the protruding areas of the inner ring so that the top and bottom are smooth. If necessary, clean up any solder bits from the middle area.

2. Flux all around each of the outer rings and place paillons of hard or medium solder around the top and bottom areas of the outside of the ring. If hard solder is used, the previously soldered joins should be refluxed and a paillon of hard solder placed on or near them again.

5. The base of the collet is now filed, ready to be soldered to the ring. Hold it on an oval file and file in a straight line to give it a curve.

soldering operation. The binding wire thus holds the previously soldered collets firmly whilst the new one is being soldered on. The same grade solder can be used throughout, and it is advisable to reflux the soldered settings as well as the new one.

Alternatively, the decorative pieces can be filed to fit the curve of the ring and then have a wire, of approx. 1–1.5mm diameter, soldered onto the back of each one with hard solder.

A hole is drilled through the ring, which is countersunk, so that the wire on the back of the decoration fits tightly into it. Easy solder is then used to fix the decoration onto the ring and the wires protruding on the inside can be cut out or filed away. See drawing below.

6. After the base has been filed to fit the curve of the ring, use binding wire to hold it in the correct position for soldering. Flux the area of the join and place paillons of easy solder down into the collet so that they are touching the area where the ring and collet meet. After soldering, the ring is polished ready for the stone to be set.

Sometimes a ring like this has several stones or other decorative pieces which are soldered around the band at equal intervals. To do this, the place where the fitting is to go should be marked out carefully with dividers, and each collet or decorative piece should be filed to fit the curve of the ring. These are then soldered on individually, held by a new piece of binding wire for each

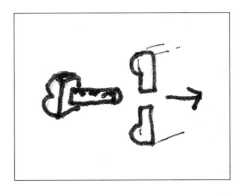

4. Hollow Ring

Textured hollow ring set with flourite.

A hollow ring enables you to construct a larger ring of any shape you want but that is not necessarily very heavy. The basic shape of the ring is defined by the outer strip, which can be curved and tapered as desired. The ring shown here uses a very simple outer shape, but the principles are the same, whatever the shape. If you are setting a stone similar to the one shown above, make the collet first.

MATERIALS
Silver sheet 0.7mm approx. 10cm x 10cm.
Silver sheet 1mm approx. 10cm x 5cm, enough for the ring size.
Silver or gold sheet for collet, 0.5mm.
Faceted stone. The one shown is a flourite.

The outer shape of this ring is somewhat dictated by the size of the stone. The top of the ring has to be big enough for the collet to fit neatly onto it.

Before bending up the shape required for this ring, I textured the surface of the silver, by placing cotton wool on one side of the metal and rolling them together through a rolling mill.

1. Bend up the outer shape of the ring. To make a sharp corner at each end of the top, mark where the inside of the bend will be with a scriber and then use a triangular file to file a groove along the marked line. Ideally the depth of the groove should be just more than half the thickness of the metal. Use a pair of flat-nosed pliers to make the bend.

Run some hard solder into the bends.

2. Join the shape at the bottom end of the ring, and then taper it with a flat file down towards the bottom so that it becomes a wedge shape.

3. Mark the area for the collet and, if the stone has a deep base, cut it out to give the stone room to sit down into it.

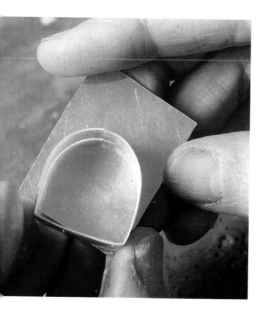

4. Place the shape onto the 1–1.5mm sheet.

5. Flux the join and place paillons of hard solder around the edge and solder together. After pickling and rinsing, cut the excess silver away from the outside edge.

6. Now make the inner ring to the desired size. The width should be the same as the widest part of the outer ring. File a similar taper on one side down towards the join and place it inside the outer ring and onto the backing sheet. Position it as desired within your outside shape. Solder the ring to the backing sheet.

7. After pickling and rinsing, drill a hole through the backing sheet, near to the inner ring, thread the piercing saw blade through it and cut out round the circle.

8. File a taper on the protruding side of the inner ring to exactly the same shape as the outer ring.

This side is then placed onto more silver sheet 1–1.5mm and soldered on.

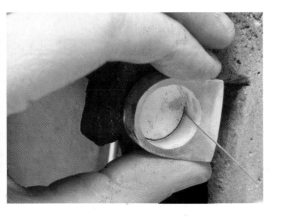

9. Drill another hole close to the inner ring as before, and pierce out the sheet inside.

10. After cutting away the excess silver from around the outside, file both the outer and inner sides so that they are flush with the original shape, and clean up the ring with wet and dry papers. The setting is now soldered to the ring over the space cut out for the stone.

11. If the stone being set does not require the cut-out space in the outer ring, two small holes should be drilled as close as possible to the edge of the collet

Before soldering the setting for the stone to the ring, the two little holes are drilled as close to the proposed edge of it as possible, so that they will not be noticed through the transparency of the stone. Alternatively the holes can be drilled on the underside of the ring. They are necessary to prevent the possibility of the ring exploding during the last soldering. The ring is pickled after soldering on the setting. It should then be given a good rinse in water and be heated again, very gently, so that the remains of the water and pickle can be expelled before the ring is finally finished.

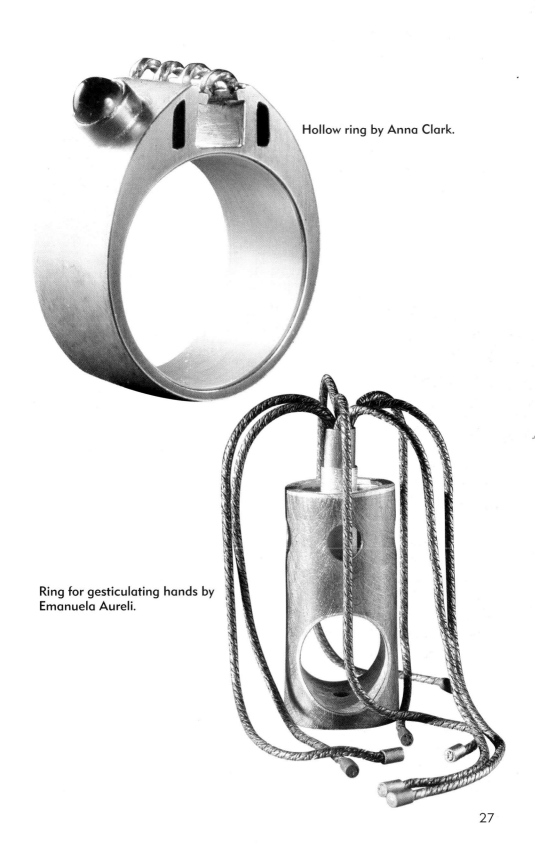

Hollow ring by Anna Clark.

Ring for gesticulating hands by
Emanuela Aureli.

5. Traditional Shank For Single or Multiple Stone Settings

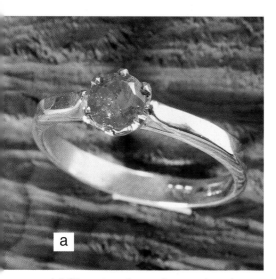

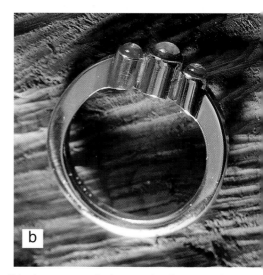

(a) Silver ring, faceted tanzanite, claw setting, (b) silver ring with three cabachon sapphires.

This is a traditional ring, which raises the stone away from the metal, to allow the light to come in from behind. As with previous rings, there are different variations on the theme and I have shown two finished rings here to illustrate two different ways of joining the shank together with the settings for the stones.

In photo (a) the square ends near the setting are cut down to divide them in two and, in photo (b) the square ends are flattened to bring them elegantly up to meet the settings. Traditional 'open' collets as in ring (a) for faceted stones can be purchased from your bullion dealer or most jewellery tool suppliers. Alternatively, you can make your own (see chapter 2 mount 5, page 77).

The collets in ring (b) are made with tube or chenier for cabochon stones. If you prefer the 'closed' look for a faceted stone, make the cone shape as described in chapter 2, mount 5 and solder that to the shank.

MATERIALS
Silver wire 2.5 or 3mm square section approximately 55mm long.
Silver sheet 0.5mm. 30mm x 30mm is plenty big enough for a stone of 6mm diameter.
Silver wire 1mm round. 50mm.
Faceted tanzanite 6mm diameter.

The square wire for this ring is forged and filed in the middle so that it becomes slightly D shaped, while the two ends remain square.

1. This can be done, either by placing it in a swage block as shown and shaping it down until it takes the curve of the block or, by thinning and rounding it by forging the central area on a flat stake.

2. File the shaped central area to neaten it.

Anneal the silver as necessary whilst forging.

The forging increases the length of the wire, so check the measurement required for the ring until the desired length is reached, or if necessary trim the square ends to shorten the length.

The ends are now brought together to be soldered.

As the square section's ends are more difficult to curve than the forged middle section a 'former' is used to help them round. This can either be done by placing the former and the wire in a vice or, by putting the wire on some soft paper on a 'lead cake' and placing a piece of round steel squarely across the silver, as shown.

3. The steel is then hit directly with the flat face of a hammer which causes the softer silver to curve up round the former.

Don't be tempted to use your steel punches as a former to do this. The marks made by the hammer hitting the steel can be considerable and the punches are too precious to hit like this!

The ring is now soldered and rounded on the mandrel to get the correct shape, and then cut open again, through the soldered line.

4. A line is now cut down the middle of the square ends. Use a pair of dividers to mark the middle line.

5. You will need to cut about 4–5mm down, which is enough to bend the silver into a nice curve which sits neatly up to the collet. Use a pair of half-round pliers to curve the top pieces back.

File the saw marks on both ends and clean them with wet and dry papers.

The underpiece, which keeps the circular shape of the ring, is now cut back and shaped for the collet to be slotted and soldered in.

In ring (b)

Before cutting it through the soldered join the square ends are flattened by forging them with a flat-headed hammer on a flat stake, or by using a rolling mill to flatten just the top area of the ring. As this will distort the circle, anneal the ring after flattening and round it up again on the mandrel.

6. The collet that is being soldered into the ring is placed against the flattened area and lines are marked which follow the line of the collet. You can use a marker pen for this. Cut through the ring where you have marked it. (I like to cut through just short of the line and then file to get an exact fit.)

7. The collet is then soldered in. There should be enough tension in the ring to hold the collets tight for soldering. I would solder it upside down so that the shank can be supported with charcoal wedges or by holding it with sprung tweezers, so that there is no movement as it is being heated.

6. Curved Hollow Ring For Large and Small Stones

a

b

(a) Curved hollow ring set with cabachon sapphire and (b) curved hollow ring set with labradorite.

This ring builds up a hollow area to allow for a large or small stone to be set.

I have used ring (a) for this demonstration. The formula for working out the lengths involved is shown below. There is scope for fancy piercing work around the shoulder area as you will see once you have found how it all curves up into shape. In picture (b) I used half-round wire to set the stone and this process is described in chapter 2, mount 3.

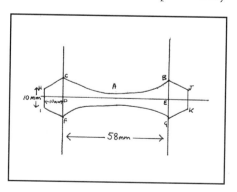

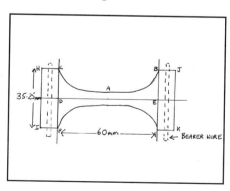

Pattern 1 is for Ring a and Pattern 2 is for ring b.

In ring (a) the cone shape is continuous so that the stone sits neatly at the top. The formula for both shapes is the same. It also has an inside ring so that the interior cannot be seen. These types of rings are often made without the inside ring to keep them lighter as, when making something in an expensive material such as gold, the weight does have to be taken into account.

To draw these patterns for hollow rings you need to know: the length of the ring and the circumference of the stone or other, being set in the top. In the drawings on the previous page, the length of the ring required is 58mm and 60mm respectively. This is shown by the lines D–E. The circumference of the stone is shown by the lines C–F and B–G.

The curved line, A–B–C shows the shape we want the ring to be and which allows for enough silver to set the stone. So, effectively, the curved line is the length required for the ring.

This presents a little problem! However, we can deal with it in one of two ways. Looking at the drawing, we can see that there is a difference between the length of the line D–E and the line A–B–C. We can either ignore this and cut out the pattern as we have drawn it, and after we have bent it up to shape and soldered it together, we can adjust the size by removing a small piece from the back of the shank. Alternatively, we can cut a piece of binding wire the actual length required and lay it out in a curve

before drawing the pattern. This will result in the line D–E being shorter.

It is very difficult to be accurate with the sizing of this type of ring, so the final adjustments can be made when the ring is shaped and soldered.

The lines C–F and B–G are 10mm and 35.25mm respectively and are equal to half the circumference of their stones. (As usual, when making up a band, the thickness of the metal used is taken into account. The metal here is 0.5mm thick so I have added 1mm to the length of the circumference of each stone.) The horizontal and sloping lines H–I and J–K which go beyond the ring length show the height required, for these particular rings, above the finger.

The circumference of a round stone is diameter x pye. The value of pye is either 3.142 or $^{22}/_7$. The circumference of an oval stone is length plus width ÷ 2 x pye.

MATERIALS
Silver sheet 0.5mm–1mm x 90mm
   x 50mm.
(If the ring is to have an interior ring, sheet of 0.5mm would be suitable. Without an interior ring, I would suggest at least 1 mm thick.)
Silver wire 1.5mm x 50mm bearer
   wire.
6mm round cabochon sapphire.

Having drawn the pattern for your ring, trace the outline carefully onto a piece of tracing paper. Glue the complete piece of paper onto the silver sheet and pierce carefully around your traced line.

Anneal the cut out silver, pickle and rinse.

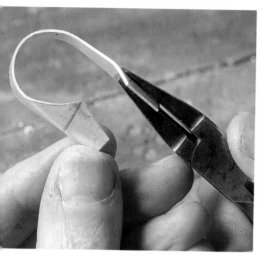

1. Using the half-round pliers, bend the ring into shape.
Use hard solder to solder both sides together.

2. I used the 'stick' soldering technique here as the line to be soldered is quite long.

The joins are fluxed as usual and a long thin strip of fluxed solder is held with tweezers. The ring is heated as normal and at the point where the solder would flow, the stick is introduced to the join. I usually place one or two paillons of solder on the join so that I can see clearly the moment to introduce the stick solder.

Pickle and rinse the ring and file the joins clean.

3. Shape the top of the ring to the shape of the stone. Here I used a small round former (which just fitted inside) and gently tapped around it.

4. Shape the ring on the mandrel carefully so that it does not distort. If you are using an oval stone, form the basic shape before soldering and make any adjustments with the half-round pliers afterwards.

We now have to make a shoulder as a base support for the stone. This is called a 'bearer' wire. Using the 1.5mm silver wire make a small ring with an outside diameter wider than the stone, and an inside diameter less than the stone, thereby creating a ledge for the stone to sit on. If necessary flatten the ring a little on a steel surface.

5. Flux the area inside the main ring and place the 'bearer' in from behind. Make sure it is sitting straight. Use medium solder to fix it in place.

6. The ring is now ready to have an inside ring fitted if desired. Trim the main ring with an oval file so that

the interior ring fits snugly into it. Make the interior ring slightly wider than the widest part of the main ring and push them together.

7. Flux both sides of the ring and place paillons of easy solder around both sides. Be fairly generous with the solder as it will take a fair amount to solder all round both sides.

After soldering, the excess silver is cut away and the ring is filed, and cleaned with wet and dry papers. The top is filed so that the stone sits at the correct height. See chapter 3, setting 1(b), page 91.

For ring (b), the procedure is exactly the same. The area for the stone of course will be much larger and will therefore require a larger bearer wire for the stone to sit on. Alternatively, this can be soldered on before the ring is bent into shape.

7. Tension Setting

Oval wire ring with faceted tourmaline.

Stones which are 'tension' set have a lovely minimal sort of quality about them. They also beguile one into thinking it's all very easy, but the same amount of thought and planning applies here as everywhere else!

Choosing the metal to match the stone is very important. The width must be just wider than the length or diameter of the stone and the thickness must be just more than the height of the stone, from the table to the culet. See page 69.

The slots, which are cut and filed into the ring, locate the stone in its correct position, but effectively the position is held by the tension in the circle of the ring. As silver is a relatively soft metal, small section silver is not really suitable for a tension setting. Choose a metal which hardens easily when worked over a mandrel such as 9 carat gold and platinum, or by using a silver or 18 carat gold thicker than usual, which will make it more difficult to spring apart.

MATERIALS
Silver oval section 7mm x 4mm x 700mm+
Faceted tourmaline length 6mm height 3mm, width 5mm

Cut the oval silver to the exact length of the ring required and file the ends straight if necessary. Anneal the piece.

1. Place a steel former in the safe jaws of a vice and tighten it up gently whilst holding the end of the oval wire against it. Keep the wire at 90° to the former and pull it carefully down over it.

Do the same thing with the other end of the wire. This should start to bring the two ends close together. To assist in getting them to sit closely, move the former along the vice so that an end protrudes beyond it and then hold the silver over the middle and push down both sides.

2. When the two ends are nicely together, solder them with easy solder. Round up the ring over the mandrel and, if necessary, work harden it at this stage, by hitting carefully with a polished flat-headed hammer. Unwanted marks made by the hammer can be removed by filing them or planishing them out with a planishing hammer.
Check for size at this point.

Hammering with a metal hammer is likely to increase the size of the ring, so allowance for this can be made when determining the size of the ring.

3. Clean the ring and finish it with the wet and dry papers, and polish if desired. Assuming the width at the girdle of the stone is 5mm, the slot for it to sit in must be just less than that, so that it will be held under tension. As a tourmaline is not a super hard stone like diamond, it should have slightly less pressure applied than would a diamond. It follows therefore that the amount of silver that is cut away is critical!

4. Mark the centre line, where the join has been made, with a scriber. Measure 2mm either side of the line and mark both lines. Make a mental note of where you think the centre point inside the circle of the ring would be and cut through the ring on both sides following that imaginary line to the centre, i.e. like making a slice in a cake (see below).

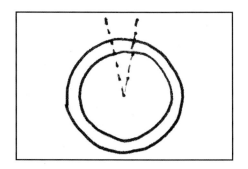

Allowing for the top of the stone to be fractionally below the top surface of the ring, a mark is made, on either side of the ring that has been cut open, to show the position of the girdle of the stone.

6. Offer up the stone at intervals to check that the angles you are filing match those of the stone.
The stone should at all times be just a little wider than the gap you are working on.

5. A groove is made along this line with a needle file. Here I used a triangular file, as the profile resembled that of the stone. Care is needed to make sure that the top edge of the ring is not filed back too much when filing the groove for the stone.

Continue until you are confident that the stone will fit into the slot you have made and it is cleaned up nicely. The area under the groove is filed as necessary for the stone to fit comfortably.

Now just open up the ring a little, either by pushing it gently down a mandrel or with a little pressure in your hands and slip the stone into the slot. It will need to be secured with raised grains at both ends. See chapter 3, setting 5.

Rough-cut stones, tension-set in gold and silver, by Barbara Christie.

8. Cast Rings

a

b

Signet-type ring set with faceted sapphire (a).

Carved signet ring with enamel insert (b).

In this section we just touch on some of the many possibilities to be considered when choosing to make a ring by casting. I will not go into the detailed methods of casting here, for further reading see the Bibliography. What we are doing here is building a ring, which is suitable to be cast, and using casting as the method of producing a ring which would be impractical to make in any other way.

c

Wrapped silver ring (c).

When making or planning a piece for casting, give yourself an extra 10% when sizing. The piece to be cast will be approximately 10% smaller than the original model.

So, when making an original in wax which will then become the 'master' for further casting, allow for an approx 20% reduction.

If you have access to good casting equipment and a kiln, you can cast any of the rings described here, yourself. I have ended each description at the point of casting.

Ring models can be made in many mediums. The most usual is a wax of some sort, which either makes a one-off piece where the wax is lost in the burn out, or the metal result from the 'lost' wax is refined and itself becomes the 'model' or 'master' for further rings of the same design. Anything that burns out completely inside the plaster mould in the kiln is suitable for making a model.

A carved, waxed signet ring
Ring (b)

Ring-shaped waxes can be purchased in lengths of approximately 100mm. They are either blue or green and have a hole running through the centre, which is equivalent to a small ring size.

1. A 'coping' saw or ordinary piercing saw with a blade size 00 will cut through the wax with ease.

Wax can be shaped and filed with any of your metal working tools. The wax will clog up the files and blades very quickly so take the time to clear it away. Green waxes are harder than blue although both are suitable for shaping, filing, piercing and heating.

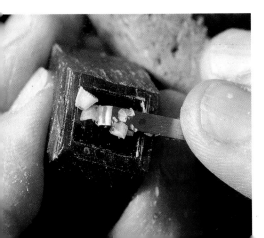

In ring (b) I carved the shape from green wax and used an engraving tool to carve out the top of the ring for the enamel piece to be set into. I attached a wax sprue to the heaviest part of the wax, i.e, the shoulder. The 'sprue' is the channel through which the molten metal passes on it's way from the crucible to the ring. After it is cast refinements are made to the silver ring and, if it is to be used as a 'master' for further castings it is given a polished finish and a brass sprue attached to the shoulders.

2. This green wax, which is fairly hard, can be chiselled out with an engraving chisel, as accurately as you like.

Building up the ring in silver for a master. Ring (a)

Making the 'master' in metal cuts out the first stage of making it in wax. Thicknesses can be built up in one area of a ring without having to make the whole piece out of impossibly thick material.

MATERIALS

Silver sheet 1mm–1.5mm thick depending on the thickness of base shank that is required, enough for wide rings.

Make up the first ring so that it is slightly bigger than you want it, to allow for the shrinkage. About one size up is usually sufficient.
Make a second ring big enough to

allow the first ring to sit just inside it. You can get the measurements to do this accurately by tying binding wire round the outside of the first ring, cutting it open, measuring the length and adding on twice the thickness of the metal. Cut a section out of the second ring to attach to the top of the first. I would suggest about half of it.

File the top on the ends of your section so that they come to a fine point. This helps integrate the section onto the first ring when they are soldered together. With the remaining half of the second ring, a further addition to the height can be made. Open it out slightly on a former or mandrel so that it sits neatly on top of the first section. Trim the ends back a few millimetres and file the tops of the ends down to a point again. Turn both sections over and cover the undersides with flux.

up and allow the solder to run. Pickle well and rinse. Use an oval file to remove the lumpy tops from the solder.

2. Cover the underside of the two sections with flux and fasten them tightly to the main ring with binding wire. Place some paillons of the same solder around the outside edges of the sections and the ring where they meet.

Solder it all together and give it a good pickle before rinsing.

1. Cut paillons of hard or easy solder and place several evenly distributed pieces on both sections. Heat them

3. The ring is then shaped with a fairly coarse file before getting it to its final shape with finer files and wet and dry paper.

4. A metal sprue is now soldered to the heaviest part of the ring.

The model is polished finally before it is sent to be cast.

Using Wax Sheet. Ring (c).

The model for this ring was made with wax sheet, cut with a craft knife into a long tapered strip.

A warmed steel jig, wiped with a little oil, was used to ease the tapered wax round the former, and then slide it smoothly off.

The wax was then filed to clean away any lumps left from heating and joining it.

A wax sprue was attached to the heaviest part of the ring. It was then ready for casting.

Little tools used for clay modelling can be used when making wax models. Joins in the wax are made with a warmed tool which has been heated by holding it over a small flame for a second or two. Waxes can be bought in strips, similar in section to silver wire. Electric pens, which dispense hot wax, are also

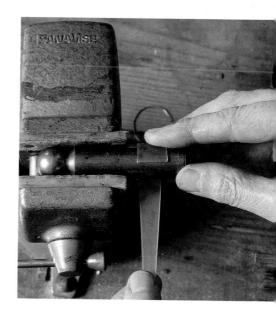

available which can give a very fluid like appearance when applied on top of a base sheet of wax.

Cuttlefish casting/sandcasting

A cuttlefish can be used, either to make an impression of a model, or be carved out to the pattern required. Molten metal is poured directly into the cavity to produce the finished article. In a similar operation, dense sand especially produced for casting is used to make the impression of a model and metal is cast directly into it.

Lost wax

The model is made in wax. The wax is suspended in a plaster casting which, when dried, remains stable in a hot kiln, allowing the wax to burn out from it. Molten metal is then forced in to the cavity, usually centrifugally, to make the final article. (These articles, can become the 'master' for many identical pieces.)

Rubber Mould

A mould of rubber is constructed around the 'master'. This is expertly cut in half to remove the master, leaving a cavity within the rubber mould. Hot wax is injected into the rubber mould, which takes only a few seconds, and the many identical waxes are then mounted all together on a wax tree, which is then encased in a plaster and burnt out in a kiln as for the Lost Wax. Many identical items are produced in this way, usually by commercial casters.

Carved insects on rings by Chris Hawkins.

9. Russian Wedding Rings

Traditionally these rings are made with three coloured golds with D section wire. White, red and yellow gold is available in most carats and these are the colours which are usually used. The idea is for the three rings to 'roll' down the finger and despite the triple thickness, be very comfortable to wear.

MATERIALS
D section silver wire 2mm high x 4mm wide x 250mm length.

Assessing the correct size for Russian wedding rings is different from sizing an ordinary ring. Not only does the height of the D section have to be taken into account, but the other two bands have to be allowed for as well.

The sample measurements are for a finger size 'O', but they can be applied in exactly the same way for other sizes. The length for O is 58mm and 4mm is added to this length to allow for the height (2mm) of the D section which makes the length approx. 62mm.

A further 2mm plus 2mm is added to allow for the thickness of the two other rings which is 66mm. This means the length of each ring is 66mm.

Cut three equal lengths from the D section wire and straighten up the ends if necessary with a file.

Anneal the three pieces before bending.

Bend each ring individually and solder it up with hard solder. Pickle and rinse. Round them all up on a mandrel and make sure they sit flat, by tapping them on a flat steel sheet.

File away any excess solder and clean all the rings on the inside as well as the outside with wet and dry papers, so that they will need minimum finishing when they are all together.

1. Make a neat cut through the solder join on two of the rings.

2. Open one of those rings with a sideways action using a pair of flat-nosed pliers in either hand and holding the ring at either side of the cut you have just made. Twist one hand towards you and the other away. This will open the ring

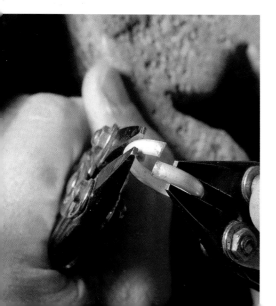

without ruining the circle you have just made on the mandrel.

Slip the ring you did not cut through the gap and close it up again using the same twisting action with the pliers.

Flux the join on this ring and place another little piece of solder across it and solder it up. Make sure there is no flux touching the other ring and that the join on the other ring is not laid too close to the join you are soldering.

3. The third ring is now opened in the same way as the second and the other two together are slipped into it. Close up the third ring and just try rolling it down your finger. If it doesn't run smoothly, take the two joined ones out again and put them in the other way round.

Solder up the third ring as you did the second. The rings are now cleaned up with wet and dry papers and polished on a mop or tumbled in a barrel polisher.

10. Curved & Anticlastic Shapes

There are two types of curve that can be applied to a simple ring band. The first is a 'synclastic' curve, which is shaped with both curves orientated in the same direction. The second is an 'anticlastic' curve, which is shaped with the curves orientated in opposite directions. After these initial shapes have been tried and tested, the wonderful possibilities, for interesting and unusual shapes which lend themselves to different textures and finishes, will emerge. The synclastic shape is easily made over a rounded stake. The anticlastic shape will need a stake with a depressed curve and a diameter suitable for holding a ring over. For further reading on the principles of both synclastic and anticlastic raising I would suggest *Form Emphasis for Metalsmiths* by Heikka Seppa, Kent State University Press.

These sorts of curves are very familiar to the silversmith. They are used frequently for such things as spouts for coffee and tea pots, and sculptural forms in table and church ware.

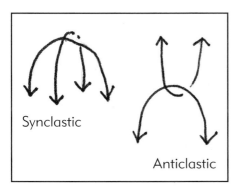

Synclastic

Anticlastic

With both the synclastic and anticlastic rings, I would suggest starting with the band a little bigger than you need. With the first one, the edges are being compressed in and, if despite that, the ring is fractionally too big, it can always have the edges compressed more, or have a small section cut out of it. Similarly, with the second ring. As metal is compressed into the centre, it could become smaller than intended, even allowing for the fact that the edges are being stretched.

It is much easier to remove a piece from either ring than it is to add one! See sizing rings, page 108.

Synclastic ring

MATERIALS
Silver sheet 0.6mm approx 70mm
  x 10mm.
You will also need: a round-headed stake which will fit inside the ring.

Make up a fairly wide band silver ring in 0.6mm thickness. The edges

of the ring are coaxed towards each other, whilst the centre of the ring is coaxed out away from them.

Make sure the ring is annealed well before starting work over the stake.

Work one edge at a time. Hold the ring so that one edge is in contact with the round head of the stake.

1. Use a clean flat-headed, fairly light hammer to tap the edge against the stake, whilst turning the ring steadily round it.
There should be a direct line of contact between the hammer head, the ring and the stake.

2. Gradually bring the ring further over the stake, working in the same way until the centre of the ring is reached.

Anneal the ring again when necessary to keep it easy to work.

Put the ring back on the stake the other way round to work the other edge.

If a steeper curve is required, the ring should be worked over a smaller-headed stake. Work mainly around the middle area to push it out more.

When the desired shape is reached the ring can be planished (see Finishing, page 105) or cleaned with a needle file and wet and dry papers.

You may decide to solder in an interior ring. This does finish the overall shape of the ring neatly. The interior ring can also be 0.6mm, but thicker can be used if required for the sizing.

Anticlastic ring

MATERIALS

Silver sheet 0.8mm or 1mm, approximately 70mm x 10mm.

Silver chenier 10mm (if setting a stone).

Cabochon black onyx (bullet type shown here) with base diameter just larger than the *inside* diameter of the chenier.

You will also need:

A steel 'sinusoidal' stake or a stake made from either steel, wood or plastic, with rounded 'hills and valley', filed into it, but over which the basic ring can pass.

A 'wedge' shaped hammer with an unmarked 'U' section end. This could be either steel, wood or plastic. A plastic or wood hammer will mark the silver less than a steel one.

Make up your silver band. Hold the stake in the safe jaws of a vice and hold the ring in your hand over the curve you wish to follow.

replaced. The same passes are made along the other side.

4. After the ring has been worked over completely once, it will need annealing. When it is soft again, tighter curves may be achieved by working over tighter curves in the stake.

5. Once the shape required has been reached it can be planished or filed to help remove any marks, or filed to remove them. Clean through the central area of the ring with wet and dry papers.

The edges of an anticlastic ring are accentuated by polishing them with a burnisher (see page 108).

The base of the chenier for the setting is filed to match the curve which has formed in the middle of the ring. This is a completely opposite curve from that normally required to solder collet onto a ring.

Hold the chenier in the correct position for soldering with binding wire, and use easy solder.

See setting 1(d), page 92.

1. Hold the ring between the thumb and forefinger of the hand not being used to hold the hammer and from the underside of the stake.
The hammer is struck onto the metal just lower than the direct line of contact with the stake as this helps to compress the metal into the centre.

2. Passes with the hammer are made round the complete circumference of the ring, working from the edge to the middle, until the curving starts to happen.

3. The ring is then taken off the stake, turned around and then

11. Fusing and Texturing

Although I am only using one ring here, to show both techniques, each one in itself is a fascinating subject. With bold experimentation, there is a lot of fun to be had with these techniques and, although there may be some failures along the way, the ones which are successful, will be well worth the effort.

Fusing

The art of fusing, is raising the temperature of the metal so that the surface just starts to liquify prior to melting. At this point, it becomes possible to fuse silver to silver, or gold to silver, or gold to gold.

SILVER

When fusing silver to silver, start off with a piece that is bigger than you want the finished piece to be.

Flux all the areas that are to be joined together. When fusing wire and flat pieces onto sheet, there should be a good area of contact between them. If parts of the wire stand away from the sheet, the raised part will melt before the rest has fused. In some cases this may be the effect wanted, but melted wire can very quickly become too messy. After fusing, the silver is brittle and also somewhat porous, so after it has been thoroughly pickled and rinsed, I always anneal the piece again before starting to work with it.

If the piece has started to melt badly at the edges, it becomes more difficult to bend up into a ring.

Instead of working on a flat strip, try working with a ring which is already formed, but not soldered.

Bend up a basic ring. I do not solder this ring as the temperature required for fusing is higher than that required for soldering, and if there is solder present in anything being fused it will burn out. The area of the join however, should fit really closely so that it will fuse together easily. Wires, and pieces of scrap silver can now be wrapped into and around the base ring. Make sure that there are plenty of points of contact all around and flux the whole ring.

Bring in the flame, gently at first to allow the water in the flux to bubble without upsetting the outside pieces. Bring the work up to the temperature required for hard soldering until it appears quite red. Watch carefully for signs of change in the surface of the silver. As it starts to fuse it becomes shiny. Hold this temperature steady and pass the flame round the whole piece, (watching as you turn) the fusing happening on one section at a time.

Do not increase the temperature at all during the fusing stage, otherwise everything will start to melt and become a big molten ball. The fusion should be reasonably controlled. You may have to keep flicking the flame away to remove the direct heat as you see surfaces altering, but it should be brought back again to continue the fusing.

After pickling and rinsing, anything which has not worked well can be redone, but it must be fluxed again. When the piece is clean, odd pieces which look wrong can always be cut out or filed to make them fit into the overall shape. Other pieces, this time soldered in, may be added to complete the ring.

As fusing increases the porosity of the metal, it is advisable to place it into a solution of hot soda salts and water, after pickling. (Rinse in water first.) This will neutralise any traces of pickle. Use some pummice powder and water paste to scrub the piece thoroughly before finishing.

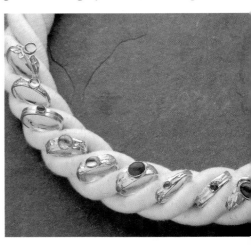

Rings formed by fusing, Jinks McGrath.

GOLD to SILVER
If your work is to be hallmarked it is very important that the amount of gold added to anything silver weighs less than the silver. If the gold weighs more, it is then viewed the other way round, i.e. that silver has been added to gold which devalues

the gold and is therefore not of hallmarkable quality.

Do not use low carat golds to fuse to silver. The gold has a tendancy to eat down into the silver and more or less disappear! It can also leave holes, so unless that is the effect required, don't use it! Low carats can be soldered to silver. But again, it can start to sink into the silver, so be careful not to overheat it.

I like to use 18, 22 or 24 carat when fusing gold to silver.

1. As when fusing silver, flux the gold first before laying it onto the silver. Very thin gold can be used to make sure that neither the weight or the cost becomes prohibitive.

As the gold has a higher melting temperature than silver, only the silver surface will start to shine when the correct temperature is reached. This is enough for the silver to 'grab' the gold from underneath and fuse them together.

Occasionally, the silver will 'spill' over onto the gold and almost obliterate it. If this does happen, it can be removed by giving the piece a quick dip into nitric acid, or by physically removing it with an engraver or fine file.

Silver rings with fused gold foil.

2. Very fine gold foil can also be fused onto silver.

3. The foil is placed between two sheets of tracing paper and the pattern cut out with a craft knife or sharp scissors.
It is then lifted onto the silver on the end of a moist paintbrush and held down with a little saliva. Sounds silly, but it works! Saliva is just what is needed to hold the foil on the silver. The silver is gently heated (the flame should not directly touch the foil) until is a faint red, which is

flame is moved carefully along or around the piece, removing it quickly if it starts to look too hot. It is pickled and cleaned in the usual way.

Texturing

There are many different ways to introduce an interesting texture onto a ring. The simplest is to use a planishing or ball pein hammer. The finished ring is placed onto the mandrel and small, even, direct hits are made all over it with the hammer. A texture can also be made with the use of a pendant motor. There are several different little heads to fix in the chuck, which will give a variety of textures. It is advisable to try these out on scrap pieces of metal first to see different looks and assess the suitability.

Other textures should be applied before the ring is soldered together, so minimum filing and cleaning is designed into the ring at this stage. A rolling mill, used with anything less hard than itself against the metal being textured is excellent for this. Stainless steel sheet can be used, but hard wire should not. Standard silver should be annealed and pickled at least three times before being textured through the mill. This softens the surface of the silver, thus allowing a stronger imprint of the texture or pattern.

Copper and gold should also be in an annealed state before texturing through the mill.

approximately 600°C (1112°F) annealing temperature. The flame is removed at this point and a steel burnisher is used to rub the foil firmly down onto the silver.

It can then be pickled in the usual way, but it should not be filed or subject to wet and dry papers. It follows therefore that when fusing gold foil to silver, that prior to application, work should be finished,

GOLD to GOLD
From 14 carat upwards, the surface of gold will start to 'shine' in a slightly more gentle fashion than silver and fusing is relatively simple. As with silver, flux should be applied to all areas to be fused, and then heated until the appearance of the surface starts to change. The

Allowances should be made for the fact that the metal, having been passed through the rolling mill, will be thinner.

Any materials with an obvious weave: imprinted paper; cotton wool; coarse wet and dry paper; string; cotton wool; coarse wet and dry paper; string; cotton, etc., are all items which will leave a good imprint on the metal. If using more than one type, they should be the same thickness, otherwise one will leave no impact as it is passed through the mill.

Silver sheet with texture from material.

To gauge the distance that the rollers should be apart to make the imprint, wind them down to where the metal just fits through and then tighten them just so that it will not. The imprint medium is then placed face down onto the metal and both are rolled through the mill.

The Ring
Textured and fused gold

MATERIALS
Strip 1mm x 15mm x 80mm
   24 carat gold (18 or 22 if fine)
0.3mm x 10mm x 10mm cut into
   shapes to be fused to the silver.
Two small lumps of potassium
   sulphide for oxidising.

Cut out the pieces of gold, flux the backs and lay them flat onto the silver. It may be necessary to anneal the gold first to make it soft enough to sit completely flat on the silver.

1. Introduce the heat carefully at first and then increase it when the bubbling from the flux has finished. Watch for the dull red to start showing in the silver and keep the flame evenly along the piece until the surface starts to glow. Move the flame along the flow of the silver as it starts to shine. If the gold looks as if it is lifting away, have a burnisher or titanium soldering stick to hand, and as the heat starts to take the gold, push it down firmly and hold it

Oxidising

Two lumps of potassium sulphide were dissolved in about half a cup of boiling water, the ring immersed until it turned black, then removed and rinsed thoroughly. Do this in a well ventilated area, it is very smelly!

I then polished the top and bottom bands, the oxidisation comes off very easily with a fine wet and dry paper,

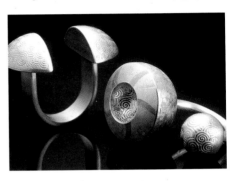

until the flame is removed.

Pickle and rinse and check to ensure that all the gold is firmly down. If not, re-fuse it!

Scrub the piece clean with pummice powder and dry it well. Place the material/paper onto the piece and pass it through the rolling mill as described previously.

2. Do any necessary filing and trimming of the strip so that it can be soldered up into a ring.
I added two square section rings to the top and bottom of this ring and filed it to shape.

It was then oxidised to make the background dark.

and the solution does not oxidise the 24 carat gold although it will darken 18 carat.

During oxidisation, the ring will appear in several different colours. If the added water is not hot enough it will take on a yellowy colour. If the water is hot, it will first appear yellowy-pink and then go to a blue-purple, finishing with deep-grey/black. To remove any of these colours the piece can be heated up again to annealing temperature and pickled.

Above: between-finger rings by Shelby Fitzpatrick. Left: silver-fused gold and oxidised silver rings by Alexandra Coppen.

12. Enamelled Rings

Silver and enamel interlocking-circles ring.

A ring which is to be enamelled has to withstand temperatures up to 900°C (1652°F) without any sort of deterioration. Fine silver 999.5, Brittania silver 955, standard silver 925, 18 carat gold and 22 carat gold can be used to make up the ring.

Neither 9 carat gold, nor platinum should be used. Enamel will not adhere to platinum and 9 carat gold does not provide a good surface for the enamel.

During construction, only enamelling solder or hard solder should be used. Solder with a lower flow point than hard will burn easily in the kiln and, if the ring is subject to several firings, I would advise using enamelling solder as it will stand up to repeated firings better than the hard.

As enamelling itself is a vast subject I will only cover the process of the firing which is applicable to this ring. Preparing a ring to be suitable for enamelling plays a crucial part in the successful outcome, so the basics shown here can be applied to other rings which are to be enamelled. See the Bibliography for books on enamelling.

18 carat gold ring with green enamel and diamonds.

Fire Scale

The fire scale found in standard silver will have an effect on transparent enamels, which causes them to become cloudy. Overcoming this fire scale problem is important, so it should be taken into consideration at the design stage.

If fine silver is used, fire scale is not present, which means that transparent colours will not become cloudy. But, fine silver is very soft and therefore, on its own, is not really a viable alternative for a ring. It could of course be strengthened with the addition of some standard silver during construction, but any exposed areas are liable to mark easily when worn.

Fire scale can be eliminated by building up a layer of fine silver on a standard silver sheet. This is achieved by annealing the piece several times and then pickling well. A 'white' surface will develop which will give a stable background for the enamels, which can either be brightened with a burnisher or cleaned with a glass brush.

The surface to be enamelled can also be 'bright cut' with an engraving tool just prior to enamelling. The tool can be used to make shapes and patterns, which add interest and brightness underneath the enamels.

MATERIALS

Standard silver, approximately
    80mm x 12mm x 1mm.
D section silver wire approximately
    2mm x 1mm x 150mm.
Silver sheet approximately
    0.5mm x 80mm x 10mm.
Burnisher.
Glass brush.
Carborundum stone.
Access to enamels and kiln.

Patterns Drawn

a

Pattern (a) is suitable for any ring size as the circles can be cut or added to without an obvious break. Pattern (b) is made specifically to fit

b

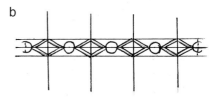

the outside of a ring size 'Q'. It could be adjusted for other ring sizes, but would need careful measuring, in order to fit the four diamond shapes accurately.

The basic ring can be made in one of two ways.

Make the basic ring and use enamelling solder to join it. Clean up the join with a flat needle file and then clean the ring right down to fine wet and dry papers.

TIP *It is easier to clean the ring at this stage, before the pattern is soldered on, than to try to clean it after the pattern has been soldered on.*

Trace the pattern onto tracing paper and stick it to the 0.5mm sheet. Drill small holes in the inside areas of the pattern and pierce them out before piercing the outside shape.

1. File all the edges to remove the piercing saw marks. It will not be possible to clean these up later.

2. Drill the holes through the circles.

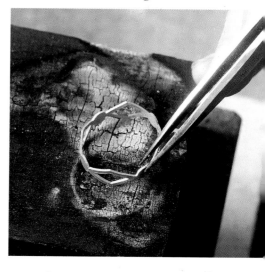

3. Bend up the pattern and solder the ends together with enamelling solder.
Round it up on the mandrel and then carefully push onto the base ring making sure it is placed in the centre.
    Make sure that the join in both the pattern and the ring are lined up and that this area is metal and is not part of the exposed area for the enamelling.

4. Cut tiny paillons of enamelling or hard solder and paint the flux carefully around the outer edges of the pattern where the solder will run.
    It is better to have more tiny paillons of solder than fewer large ones. The area to be enamelled needs to be completely free from solder.
    Alternatively, the pattern is soldered to the base before soldering it up into a ring.

TIP When tightening binding wire to a flat edge, it can be held in place by making small nicks (in an area which will be cut away) with a triangular file and using these slots to locate the wire.

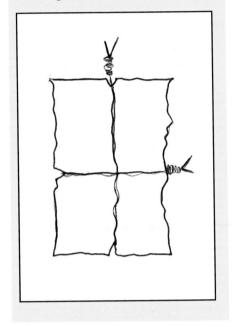

The strip of silver used for the base ring should be made completely flat and cleaned with fine wet and dry papers. It does not need to be cut to exact size at this stage. Trace the pattern and stick it to the 0.5mm silver. Drill small holes where the pattern has to be cut from the inside and pierce those areas out first. Now cut around the outside of the pattern.

Lay the pattern onto the sheet. It should be completely flat. It can be held down for soldering by fastening binding wire in three or four places along the strip.

Flux along the outside profile of the pattern and place tiny paillons of hard solder along both edges and solder the pattern to the ring base.

After pickling and rinsing, cut the ring to the exact size, making sure to allow for both thicknesses of the metal. Make sure that the join is in an area which will not be enamelled and bend the ends round so that they fit closely. Use hard solder to solder the ends together.

The same procedure now applies to both rings

File away any remains of the solder and clean up the outside of the ring.

Make up two D section rings (as in Ring 3, page 20) and use enamelling solder on each join. Solder them onto the main ring. You can use hard again at this stage. The top and bottom edges should just protrude beyond the 'D' section. This makes placing the solder easier and both rings can be soldered on at the same time.

Check to make sure there is no trace of solder in the areas to be enamelled. This can be done by heating up the ring to annealing temperature. Any residue of solder will appear black. It should be removed with either a file, engraver or small cutting tool on the pendant motor.

When the solder has been completely removed the piece should be annealed and pickled a couple of times. The area to be enamelled should be white and clean during heating.

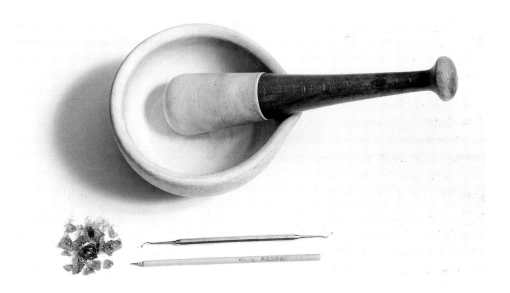

Enamelling

The area to be enamelled is cleaned by holding the ring under running water and scrubbing with a glass-brush. This leaves the surface grease free and it should not subsequently be touched with fingers.

When enamelling on standard silver, most colours will benefit from the application of a base coat or 'flux' enamel.

TIP Flux enamel should not be confused with soldering flux. It is purchased in powder or lump form and ground and washed in exactly the same way as other enamels.

It is as well to test any colour that you are thinking of using on a small sample of silver before committing it to the ring itself. Clean a small test piece of silver with the glass brush and then cover half with the flux enamel and the other half with the colours you have chosen. Fire the sample at approx. 830°C (1526°F) and make a note of any differences in length of firing times for the different enamels. You will need to bear this information in mind when firing them on the ring.

Fire the sample again, this time with the colours laid onto the previously fired flux coat. This will show the differences of a colour fired with a 'flux' background and the same colour fired directly onto the silver. Generally, it is advisable to use this initial 'flux' enamel. Reds, pinks, oranges and yellows all benefit from a 'blue flux', which is purchased as 'blue' although, when fired it is very clear with only just a hint of blue. Other fluxes such as silver flux and transparent flux are generally used with other colours.

The ring should be completely dry when laying in the enamel. The

enamel itself is 'wet packed', i.e. it is ground and washed before use and placed in a palette with some of the final rinsing water.

After the first coat of 'flux' enamel is laid in, it is allowed to dry thoroughly before firing.

This size ring will probably take one to one and a half minutes to fire at a temperature of about 850°C (1562°F). The coloured enamels are laid into the ring once the first flux and ring has cooled. Build these up in thin layers and fire each completed layer. When the enamelled area is 'full', it is rubbed down so that it is completely level with the silver surround. Hold the ring under running water and use a carborundum stone to work across the enamel, followed by 240, 400 and 600 wet and dry papers (used wet).

When the enamels are smooth, the ring is rinsed and dried and fired again for the last time to restore the shine to the enamel. The subsequent oxidisation which will occur on the silver can be removed either with the glassbrush, or by placing the ring in the pickle. (But, make sure to place your test piece in the pickle first and do not immerse the ring if the pickle adversely affects any of the colours on the test piece). Alternatively, the surface can be rubbed with a polishing paper such as 'crocus' paper which will not affect the enamel. It can also be polished with a pummice slurry or a general green polish, but this too should be tested on your test piece first.

Soldering and working platinum and gold

PLATINUM

Platinum is a heavy metal, with a specific gravity of 21.34 gm/mm3 compared with 24 carat gold at 19.5, 18 carat at 16.15, 9 carat at 12.29 and sterling silver at 9.84. It is a relatively hard metal to work and does not oxidise when heated.

Solder is purchased in small strips of hard, medium and easy. As the metal does not oxidise when heated, it is not necessary to use flux when soldering, although it will not harm if a flux is used. A much higher temperature (relative to silver and gold), of around 1400° C (2552°F) is needed to hard solder platinum. Annealing temperature is around 950–1000°C (1742–1832°F).

An oxygen-propane soldering torch is used to solder platinum as an ordinary gas torch, or gas and blown air torch, will struggle to reach the required temperature.

As the heat is so high, protective goggles should be worn which enable you to see the colour of both the flame and the metal as it reaches the desired temperature.

The join should be as close fitting as possible and a soft (not hard) hot flame is used to raise the platinum up to soldering temperature. It can be quenched immediately after soldering. The surface should remain smooth throughout all heating processes.

As platinum does not oxidise and is very strong, it is an ideal metal to use for setting hard stones such as diamonds and, as it can be polished prior to soldering it is well-suited to fine construction. The finished appearance of platinum is a steely sort of grey, but it can be brush finished to give a softer look.

GOLD

24 carat gold is such a beautiful looking metal it seems a pity not to use it for everything. But, alas, it is too soft for general jewellery purposes, so it is alloyed with other metals to give us:

Platinum ring.

22 carat	which has only 2 parts other metals
18 carat	which has 6 parts other metals
14 carat	which has 10 parts other metals
9 carat	which has 15 parts other metals

The other metals can include, silver, copper, platinum, palladium and zinc. The colour and carat of the gold depends on the quantities used of any of these metals.

Solder is purchased according to the carat of gold used. It comes in small pieces of approx. 2 x 4cm in Hard, Medium and Easy.

All joins in whatever carat of gold used should be clean and very close fitting. Gold solder will not fill gaps in the same way as silver solder can be persuaded to do.

Gold is annealed in a similar way to silver, i.e., it is heated until it takes on a deep pinkish hue. The annealing temperature varies, but is generally between 650 – 750°C (1202 – 1382°F). After annealing, different carats and colours of gold are quenched at different times. Some may be quenched immediately, others should cool down somewhat to about 500°C (932°F), whilst some are not quenched at all and allowed to cool naturally. Your bullion suppliers should be able to supply technical data for each one, but if you do not have access to this data and find that a gold remains hard after annealing, try quenching it differently.

Fluxes such as 'borax' can be used with gold, but may start to burn out at the high temperature required so a specific flux such as 'Tenacity No. 5' powder may be used. Soldering temperatures range between 650 – 860°C (1202 – 1580°F), depending on the carat of gold being used. Generally the higher the carat, the higher the temperature required for soldering.

18 carat gold downwards will all oxidise, but this can be removed in the pickle. 9 carat gold is less easy to clean well in the pickle, so after the flux has been removed, give it an extra clean with a scrub of pummice powder.

STONES CHART
pages 64-67

18 carat ring with enamel and emeralds by Jinks McGrath.

List of Stones	Colour	Location	Cut	Hardness	Associated w
Amethyst	pinky-purple	Brazil, etc.	cab/fac	7	Feb/Spring Pisces
Amythyst Cab	various	ww	cab	7	
Agate moss,	greeny-red	ww	cab	7	Gemini
landscape	paint effect	ww		7	
Alexandrite	greeny-purple/ yellow-brown	Russia etc.	fac	8.5	
Amber	orangy-yellow	Baltic area	cab	2.5	
Aquamarine	clear blue	Brazil	fac/cab	7.5	March/Aries
Azurite	blues/greens	Australia	cab	3.5	
Bloodstone	deep green & red	India	cab	7	March/Aries
Carnelian	orange-red	India	cab	7	Virgo/August
Chrysoberyl	yellow-green	Russia etc.	fac/cab (cats eye)	8.5	Spring
Citrine (quartz)	golden yellow	Brazil	fac	7	
citrine	pale yellow	Brazil	cab	7	
Diamond	clear	Australia /SA	fac	10	April/Winter
Emerald	green	Columbia	fac/cab	7.5	May/Spring Cancer
Fluorite	multi-coloured	ww	fac	4	

List of Stones		Colour	Location	Cut	Hardness	Associated with
	Garnet pyrope	strong red	USA etc.	fac/cab	7.5	Jan/Summer
	green garnet (tsavorite)	green	Kenya	fac/cab	7	
	rhodalite	purpley-red	Kenya	fac/cab	7	
	Hematite	metallic grey/ black	USA	cab	6.5	
	Iolite	bluey-violet	Sri Lanka	fac/cab	7	
	Jade, Nephrite	lavender	Burma	cab/ carved	7	
	Jadeite	dark green/ cream	Burma	cab/ carved	6.5	
	Jasper	mostly red	India	cab/ carved	7	March Mourning
	Kunzite	pink/green	Brazil	fac	7	
	Kyanite	pale/ gold patches	Burma	fac/cab	5/7	
	Labradorite	blue/green/ pinks	Labrador	cab	6	
	Lapis lazuli	blue/ gold patches	Afghanistan	cab	5.5	September
	Malachite	green black banding	Zaire	cab	4	Tradionally kept away evil Winter
	Moonstone	milkyblue/ white	Burma SL	cab	6	Passion & fortune/ Winter
	Opal	multicoloured	Australia	cab/fac	6	October
	Fire opal	bright orange greens	Australia	fac/cab	6	Summer

List of Stones		Colour	Location	Cut	Hardness	Associat
	Triplet	Colour deepened by Rock crystal on top Onyx backing	Australia	cab	6	Leo
	Onyx	brown/white/black	ww	cab	7	Winter
	Pearl	natural/pink/grey	Japan/China	natural	3	June
	Peridot	light green	China/Burma	fac/cab	6.5	August
	Quartz, rose	pink	Brazil, Madagascar	cab/fac	7	
	rutilated	visible dark flashes	Brazil, Madagascar	cab	7	
	smokey	browny	Brazil, Madagascar	cab/fac	7	
	tigers eye	yellow/brown strips	Sri Lanka	cab	7	
	Aventurine	greeny	Brazil etc.	cab	7	
	Ruby	rose red	Russia etc.	cab	9	Capricor July
	star	pinky red with 6 band white star	Burma	cab	9	Taurus/Septeml
	(varieties)	deep pink				
	Sapphire	blue (varieties) yellow, pink	Burma	fac/cab	9	Taurus/Septeml
	blue					
	green					
	large blue					

List of Stones		Colour	Location	Cut	Hardness	Associated
	Sodalite	lavender/blue	Brazil	cab	5.5	
	Spinel	red/pink	Burma	fac/cab	8	Summer
	Sunstone	orange/red	Norway/USA	cab	6	
	Tanzanite	pale lavender	Tanzanire	fac/cab	6.5	
	Topaz, yellow	pink, green	Brazil	fac/cab	8	Summer/ November
		blue				
	Tourmaline	blue/green	Russia	fac/cab	7.5	October
	watermelon	green/pink	South Africa	fac/cab	7.5	
	watermelon					
	watermelon					
	Turqouise	green/blue	Iran/Tibet/ Mexico	fac/ carved	6	Protector
	Zirconium	clear	Sri Lanka	fac	8.5	

CHAPTER 2

Mounts

Getting to know the measurements

This section is concerned with the structure of the different surrounds, usually referred to as either bezels, collets or 'mounts', and which are used to hold and display precious and semi-precious stones and/or other pieces such as enamels or found objects.

A bezel and a collet are basically the same thing. Both words refer to the piece of metal which surrounds the stone and which is bent in such a way to hold the stone securely in it.

Mounting really just refers to the action of holding the stone, however it is held. Usually, the mount is added to the ring during fabrication. Sometimes a mount is the framework that is used to hold an uncut stone, which does not have a bezel, or collet.

The objective is, that they are all made to fit the stone as closely as possible so that there is no room for movement and, that they are constructed in such a way that the shape is flattering to the stone.

The formulae listed opposite will help when calculating how much metal is needed for a mount and also with the shapes that have to be

drawn in order to make a pattern to fit some faceted stones.

When considering the type of mount to be made, you will need to be aware of the stone's vital vital *statistics*! When choosing a *cabochon* stone, you will need to know either the diameter, or length and width, or circumference. The shape of the underneath of the stone is important too. Preferably they should be nice and flat, but they sometimes have a slight curve on the base, for which allowances should be made.

With a *faceted* stone you will need to know the measurements of the diameter, or length of the sides, or circumference, plus, the height from the girdle to the table and the distance from the girdle to the culet. If the culet does not come to a point you will need to note it's width.

With some of the more complicated mounts, I often make a mock-up one first, in copper or silver so that I can make any adjustments, before making the final one in a more expensive material. It is certainly as well to cut out the shape in paper first, even if just for reassurance that what you are making bears some resemblance to the profile of the stone. The measurements should be drawn accurately onto a piece of paper and formula are used to find the shape of the metal to be cut out.

FORMULAE

(Note: add twice the thickness of the metal used for the collet to each of the following formulae:)

CABOCHON STONES
1 For round cabochon stone
Diameter x pye (pye = 3.142)

2 For oval cabachon stone
Length + Width ÷ 2 x pye

3 For square cabochon stone
Length of each side –
allowing for the corners

FACETED STONES
From the drawing you will see that the faceted stone has 1. table, i.e.

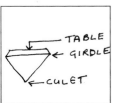

The faceted stone

the flat top area and 2. girdle, i.e. the widest edge of the stone and 3. culet, i.e. the bottom of the stone which either comes to a point or is tapered into a fine edge.

The patterns for numbers 4, 5 and 6, which find the collet shapes for different faceted stones, follow a basic principle.

A plan view of the stone is drawn first. This should show the diameter or outside measurement of the girdle

and the diameter or outside measure of the culet. The height from the girdle to the culet should also be measured and noted.

Underneath the plan view a horizontal line should be drawn. Parallel with that line, a second line is drawn, the distance between the two being the noted measurement of the girdle to the culet. A small amount of approximately 1mm should be added to this to allow for the top of the collet, or a claw to be rubbed over onto the stone.

Dotted lines are drawn vertically from each side of the girdle edge down to the first line and two more vertical lines are drawn from the edges of the culet down to the second parallel line.

The lines AB, DC are then drawn until they meet at Z, which is the center of the circle which is now drawn to find the shape.

The first circle is drawn with AZ as the radius and a second drawn with BZ as the radius. A pair of dividers is then used to measure the distance AD.

4 For the round stone
With the dividers holding the AD measurement, place one end on D and walk and mark 3 ⅓ sections on the outside circle. Draw line E-Z. The pattern for the collet is the area, darkened on the drawing here, which lies between the two circles.

The round stone

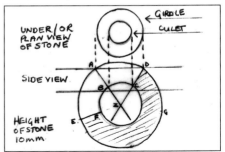

5 For the square stone

Open the dividers a fraction so that the measurement is just a little longer than AD and then walk and mark them 4 times around the outer circle. This extra length allows for the corners when you bend them up in the metal. The pattern for the collet is the area darkened on the drawing, which is made by joining straight lines between AD, DG, GH and HE and then joining BC, CI, IJ, JF.

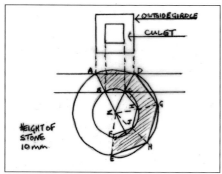

The square stone

6 For the rectangular stone

the AD mesaurement is the longer side of the stone. Open out the dividers a fraction and walk and mark 1 section on the outer circle. Measure the shorter side of the stone on the drawing with the dividers, open them a fraction and mark this measurement on the outer circle. This is repeated once more respectively. At each point GHE a line is drawn to meet at the center of the circle Z.

The pattern for the collet is the area, darkened on the drawing here, which lies between the 2 circles.

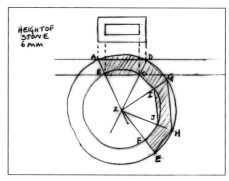

The rectangular stone

The 30mm arc

1. Draw a 30mm arc with a pair of compasses.

2. Measure the height of stone from the culet to just over the girdle and increase the compass range by that amount. Draw this arc above the first arc.

3. Calculate circumference of stone and mark the distance along the top line.

4. Join down to the centre compass point.

5. Shaded area is the flat cone to be cut and bent into shape.

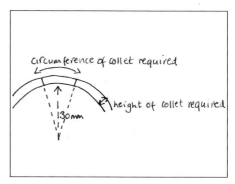

The 30mm arc

MOUNT 1
Bezal for cabochon stone
MATERIALS

Garnet ring

Cabochon garnet 6mm x 6mm
    height 4mm
Strip for Bezel: Gold or silver sheet
    0.5mm thick x 25mm long x
    2mm wide.
Silver sheet 1 x 10 x 10mm approx.

This mount, which is just a straightforward bezel soldered onto a backing sheet is for the cabochon garnet in ring 2, see page 17. As the stone has rounded corners, the bezel is also rounded at the corners. The join should be half way along one of the sides and not in a corner. This makes filing easier and allows the join to 'disappear'.

The slope and shape of the stone determine the height of the bezel. The garnet used here started to slope in about 1.5mm from the base, which

means that the bezel can be about 2mm high in order to hold the stone in firmly.

Use a pair of half-round pliers to bend the gold strip for the bezel round into shape. Offer it up to the stone as each corner is bent to check that the angle is correct.

The bezel should be fractionally long once it has been shaped, and a neat join is made by piercing a straight line through the overlapping ends and then lining them up close together.

Solder the join with gold solder. This can be either hard, medium or easy as they all have a higher melting point than silver solder. After pickling and rinsing, if necessary, file the bottom of the bezel flat on a large flat file.

Check that the stone sits in the bezel comfortably before soldering it onto the backing sheet with hard silver solder. A softer solder can be used for this, but as further solderings are required to complete the ring it is advisable to keep with the hard at this stage. The excess silver backing sheet is now filed to shape as described for ring 2, on page 17.

For a simple setting with no extra silver round the outside of the bezel, the excess silver is cut away with the piercing saw and then filed so that there is no visible line between the backing sheet and the bezel. It is then soldered to the ring shank using a softer solder.

File the top of the bezel if necessary with a flat needle file to make it even and then polish, prior to setting the stone. See settings 1, page 89.

MOUNT 2

In this mount we make a 'bearer' wire for the stone to sit on. As the mount is shaped to fit the curve of the ring, we cannot place a stone directly into it as we did in Mount 1 because the base of the stone would only touch the ring in one place, i.e. the top of the curve. If we tried to set the stone like this it would wobble all over the place. So, a flat collar is needed inside the bezel for the stone to sit on.

MATERIALS

Cabochon moonstone 8 x 8 x 5mm.

18 carat gold strip. 0.5 x 6 x 20mm.

18 carat gold strip approximately 1 x 2 x 20mm.

18 carat hard solder

TIP Gold solder is cut into very small paillons to facilitate the flow. This solder does not flow in the same way as silver, and more tiny bits along the solder line are better than fewer larger pieces. The actual join should be a very close fit.

The bezel strip is deliberately made a little longer than appears to be necessary. This is to allow for the extra thickness, introduced by the bearer wire when bending it into shape.

This inside strip or bearer wire can be made by rolling or hammering down round wire to give it two flat sides. It should remain thick enough to provide a ledge wide enough for the stone to sit on.

Make sure both pieces of gold (silver can be substituted) are completely flat.

Lay the smaller strip along the larger one. Allow 2–3 mm between the top edge of the larger strip and the top edge of the smaller. This is the approximate measurement to set the moonstone which has fairly high straight sides.

1. Flux along both sides of the small strip and place paillons of hard solder along the bottom of it. Solder them together.

2. Bend the strip to the shape of the stone. Pierce a line through both ends where they meet and solder them together.
   File and clean the join.

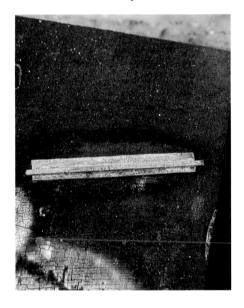

3. The bottom of the mount is then filed to fit the profile of the ring. You will need an oval file with a similar curve to the ring. The mount is filed by holding it in a straight line on the curve of the file.
Offer the mount up to the ring at frequent intervals to be sure that the filing is correct. It should sit on the ring without any gaps showing.

The mount is held on the ring with binding wire and fluxed all round the join. Silver solder paillons are placed inside the mount and tucked in closely to where the base of the mount touches the ring.

After soldering, the ring is finished and polished. There should be very little cleaning and filing to do around the base of the mount as the solder was placed on the inside and will not therefore leave solder traces around the outside. Neither will it interfere with the fitting of the stone, as the bearer wire becomes a barrier to the solder.

MOUNT 3

This setting is made using D section wire. The bezel is therefore wider than usual and looks particularly good with larger cabochon stones.

Hollow ring with labradorite

1. Choose a size of D section which is appropriate to the stone being set. For this setting I used 3 x 2mm and measured the length required by adding 4mm (which is twice the height of the D section) onto the length of the circumference of the stone. A firm line is marked on the flat side of the D which is about one third in from the edge. (Use dividers to mark this as in ring 1, page 15.)

2. Use a lozenge-shaped graver along the marked line to remove the metal to about a third of the depth.

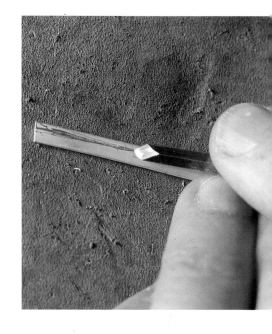

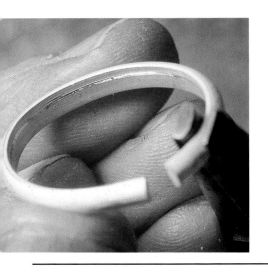

3. With the flat side of the D becoming the inside of the curve, bend up the wire to its approximate shape and solder the two ends together.

The bezel is shaped as for a round stone and then carefully squeezed together into an oval, either with a pair of parallel pliers or in the safe jaws of the vice. It is then soldered onto a backing sheet and trimmed.

To set the stone see setting Ie, page 93.

MOUNT 4

MATERIALS

Faceted tourmaline: 19 x 8mm height from table to culet 3mm
Silver sheet 1 x 20 x 15mm
 (minimum size).
Silver strip 0.7 x 50 x 4mm
Round wire 0.7mm diameter.

This mount is used to set a stone from behind instead of in front. It allows you to use shapes that would not be possible with a conventional front setting. It can also be useful if you have a lovely but rather soft stone or object to set into a ring, as the top of the setting is higher than the stone and therefore gives it some protection.

Selection of gold rings by Leslie McInnes.

Mark out on the middle of the 1mm silver sheet the exact size of the stone. Use dividers or a scribe to score the line.

Draw a second line inside the area for the stone about 1mm from the first line. On the inside of this area, drill a hole to thread the blade of the piercing saw through and then cut

2. The angled filing creates the area for the stone to sit in when held

out the middle area.

1. Use a flat file to make an angle, (which is similar to the line of the stone from the girdle to the table) along the four sides of the opening and which goes back as far as the first marked line.

upside down.

3. The front of the setting is filed and shaped.

A rectangle is now made from the 0.7mm silver strip through which the stone can pass. This mount is not shaped to follow the lines of the stone as it would be if it were being set from the front. Instead, as the stone has to fit through it before being held in, a straight-sided or slightly sloping rectangle is correct. (If the bottom of the setting is to follow the curve of the inside of the ring, add a little extra to the depth of silver required to allow for filing.) For patterns see page 82.

4. The rectangle is now soldered to the top piece. The top edge of the rectangle should sit as close as possible to the first marked line that was scribed into the top.

The mount is soldered to the ring. After pickling and rinsing, place the stone into position so that the bearer can be made. The 0.7mm silver wire is bent up and soldered into a rectangle so that it will tuck down between the edges of the stone and the inside edges of the main rectangle.

Once this is in place, grains are raised from the wall of the rectangle which hold the wire down tight against the stone. See setting 9, page 102.

MOUNT 5

Making a cone and shaping it for a basic open claw setting.

This ring has a round faceted tanzanite so I made a round cone which was filed at the top and bottom to make the claws and to allow light in from the bottom.

The pattern for making a cone is shown at the beginning of this chapter, formula for a round stone or 30mm arc. Whether the mount is kept as a plain cone and used as a rub over setting, or if it is cut and filed into a fancy collet, making the cone is the same procedure for both.

Open collets are often used with faceted stones in order to reflect as much light as possible. They are a little fiddly to make and can be bought ready-made to fit most stone sizes, from bullion and good tool suppliers. However, making one's own brings individuality to this type of setting.

Collet blocks and punches

These are steel blocks with tapered holes shaped either round, oval, square or rectangular. Each block has several of the same shaped holes, which gradually decrease in size, and one punch fits them all. They are useful to either 'true' up a collet or, if the metal is not too thick, they can shape a straight collet into a tapered one.

The collet to be shaped should fit easily inside the hole closest to its size and then be worked down as necessary. The metal should always be kept below the surface of the block, otherwise it will mark around the outside edge.

MATERIALS (Round setting)
Silver sheet 0.5 x 60 x 60mm (or whatever is appropriate to the size of your cone).
Short length of round wire 0.7–1mm.
Hard solder.
For pattern see formulae, page 69.

1. Pierce out the cone shape and bend it up with a pair of half-round pliers so that the two sides fit neatly together. It does not have to be an exact cone at this stage.

2. The cone is soldered together with hard solder.

3. Shape the cone either with the half-round pliers or using the round cone steel block. File the bottom if necessary to straighten it.

4. V-shaped grooves are now filed in the bottom of the collet cone with a triangular needle file. File opposite to opposite, so that the V goes down the sides, just enough to leave little legs for the collet to stand up steadily on, and to be decorative. Make up a little ring with the same diameter as the base of the collet using the round wire (0.7–1 mm diameter, use smaller wire for a small collet).

5. Flux and solder the ring to the base.

6. After pickling and rinsing, the top is filed flat if necessary and then marked with something like a thick blue pen either into four or five equal sections, depending on how many claws are required for the setting. The piercing saw is now used to cut down the collet equally each side of each blue line (these form the prongs which are bent over onto the stone to hold it in place.)

7. The area between the prongs is removed. This can be cut or filed out into a soft U shape and can extend down almost as far as the V-shaped groove filed in earlier.

The collet is now ready to solder into the ring shank as in ring a on page 30.

MOUNT 6

Outside claw setting for oval half-faceted tourmaline

2. Bend up the collet and solder up the join. Shape it oval, file it smooth and clean it up with wet and dry

Silver and gold ring with claw set tourmaline.

This stone is faceted from the girdle to the culet, but has a cabochon-shaped table. I have therefore built the collet to fit the shape of the stone and mounted the claws which hold the stone on the outside.

MATERIALS

Silver sheet 1 x 80 x 80mm
  (enough for cone pattern to suit
  your stone).
D section silver wire, 2 x 1mm
  approximately.
Oval tourmaline 12 x 9mm.

1. Cut out the cone for the tourmaline using the 30mm arc. The circumference length required for this stone was 35mm.

The girdle of the stone, for this setting, sits on the top rim of the collet.

papers. The stone should sit on the top edge of the collet. This can be filed to give a little slope towards the centre and to make a better fitting seat for the stone.

3. Cut four lengths from the D section for the claws. Cut them over-long, as they will be trimmed to size later.

4. Place the collet upside down on the soldering block and lay the flat side of the D section pieces against

the sides at equal distances. These can be held in place by digging them into the block. Solder one side at a time if necessary.

The bottom of the claws are filed level with the bottom of the collet. The top of the claws are cut and filed for the settings. See setting 6, page 98.

Leave approximately 2mm of claw above the top edge of the collet.

MOUNT 7
Collet for faceted rectangular flourite

There are two methods for making a rectangular or square tapered collet.

The first, (a) described here, is less exact, and therefore more suitable for stones where the cut is a little uneven. The second, (b) is shown on page 70.

MATERIALS
Silver strip: Length should be the sum total of the four sides plus twice the thickness of the silver. Height should be just more than the total height of the stone.

1. When making up a collet such as this, allow for the join to come half way along one of the longer sides. Mark out on your strip of silver where the first corner will be. From there carefully measure each side of the stone and mark on the metal where the corner will be. If the corners are rounded, allow for this. Sharp corners need to be accurately marked.

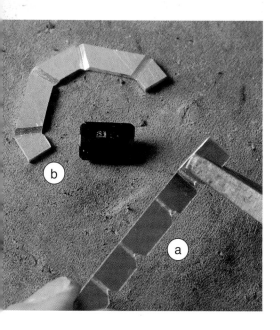

groove at the same time that you solder the side.

File to shape and solder the bezel to the ring.

The second bezel,(b) which is similar, but more exact than the one just described, is drawn out first on paper as shown in the formula. This pattern is then transferred onto tracing paper, which is stuck to the metal and cut out.

3. A groove is filed up each corner line using a triangular or square section wire.

Using a pair of flat-nosed pliers, each corner of the bezel is bent up and the join is soldered.

2. Make a small groove up each marked corner line with a triangular file.

An upside down V is cut out on the bottom edge of the collet at each corner section.

Fold each corner in with a pair of flat-nosed pliers, bringing the V cutouts in the bottom edge together.

Run some solder up each corner

TIP If a square or rectangle is joined at a corner it will appear as a slightly different shape from the other corners. Join all collets along their longer sides to avoid odd corners.

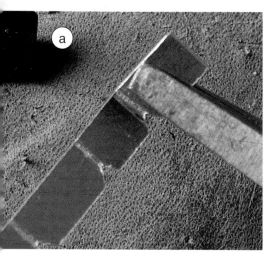

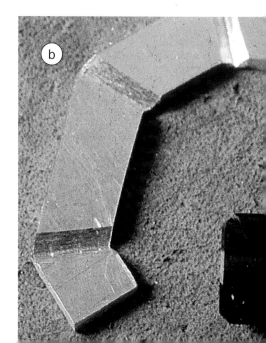

MOUNT 8

Three-sided collet for cabochon stone with an uneven back

This type of collet is suitable for either a 'claw' setting or a rub over, as I have made here. It allows light to come in from behind as well as allowing for the unevenness of the back of the stone. In this one, a seat for the stone is cut out of the sides of the bezel with a bull stick. See setting 1(c), page 92.

An alternative way of making a seat for a setting such as this, is to make up an ordinary setting for a cabochon stone, where the bezel is soldered onto a backing sheet. Most of the backing sheet is then pierced out, just leaving a little edge, wide enough for the stone to sit on, close to the bottom of the bezel.

The construction then continues as described.

MATERIALS
Silver sheet 1 x 80 x 8mm
   (or enough to cut the shape for your stone).
Silver chenier (tube). Outside diameter approximately 3mm.
Hard solder.

Draw the pattern for making the cone to fit your stone. Here, the stone is a triangular cabochon tourmaline. I cut out the length I needed from drawing the 30mm arc and adding the height required.

Tourmaline in raised setting.

As with other collets, the join comes half way down one of the sides.

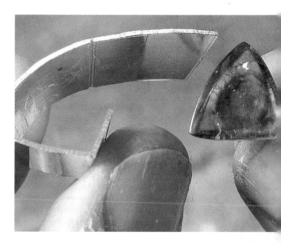

1. Mark the first corner with a scribe and file a groove along it. Bend to fit the first corner of the stone. Mark off the second corner and file a groove along it. Bend to fit the second corner of the stone.

2. Continue until you have the correct shape and run a little hard

solder up the grooves at the same time that you solder the join.

3. After pickling and rinsing, file the bottom of the collet to match the curve of the ring (if appropriate).

The centre area of the collet strip is now removed.

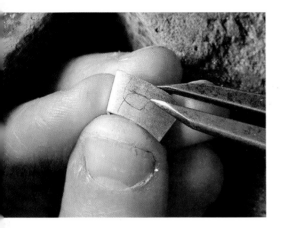

4. Mark the top and bottom lines with dividers.

5. Cut along both lines.
The two halves are now put back together again with the chenier

sandwiched in between.

6. File small round grooves, equally spaced, in the top edge of the lower half of the collet. Cut the same number lengths of chenier as grooves.
    Cut the chenier over-long at this stage. It is much easier to place them ready for soldering if they are a little longer than necessary.

7. Solder the chenier to the lower half with hard solder.
    After pickling and rinsing, file the rounded tops of the chenier so that they are a little flat.
8. Flux the chenier and sit the top half of the collet, matching the bottom half, on top of the chenier. Solder them together.
Hard solder can be used again, which allows for further soldering when the setting is soldered to the ring.
    The protruding ends of the chenier are then pierced away and the collet is filed and cleaned before being assembled onto the ring shank.

MOUNT 9

Preparing the metal for gypsy and pave settings

Sometimes a stone is set directly into the ring shank so a collet is not actually made, but an area in the ring is cut and shaped to suit the stone. The most important thing to consider when planning a setting of this sort, is the size of the stone and the size of the ring shank.

The stone must have room to sit in the ring without the culet showing through the bottom, and the metal must not fall away too rapidly (particularly at the sides of a curved ring) so that it is not able to hold the stone properly.

Having made sure that everything is the right size, the positioning of the stone is marked by a dot with the scribe. If there are several stones of the same size being set along one line, lightly mark a line with a pair of dividers, holding one side to the edge of the ring and the other side drawing the line in the centre. The dots for the drill holes can be marked by setting the dividers at the correct distance apart and marking off along the scribed line.

Flatten the top of the metal a little with a file, to give a firmer purchase when starting to drill each hole.

1. A small hole is drilled first. Do not try to drill the correct sized hole at first as a hole cut like this will usually be too big. It is better to open it out gradually.

Faceted sapphire gypsy setting.

2. A small hole can be tapered out with a special cutting head fixed in the pendant motor. These are called 'fraziers' and come in many different shapes.

A frazier can be manipulated to make a round hole oval. The hole should be the correct size for the stone to sit in, with the girdle sitting

85

just below the top surface of the ring.

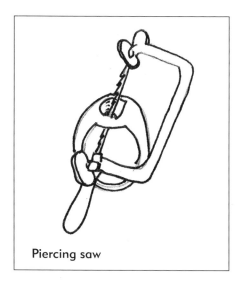

Piercing saw

Holes for square stones are drilled and then cut with the piercing saw. The initial hole is drilled and this can be opened out to a diameter about two thirds of the width of the stone. The square should then be marked around the top of the hole. The remaining area is cut out with a piercing saw. The blade is threaded through the hole and worked at an angle which cuts wider at the top than it cuts at the bottom. This should cut two sides of the square. The blade will have to be taken out and threaded through the ring from the other side to cut the other two sides. Take care not to cut into the bottom of the ring shank.

MOUNT 10

Using chenier

Chenier is used in several ways to set round cabochon or faceted stones. It can be used to set a single stone, or soldered together for multiple settings. Any side which touches its neighbour should have a little flat filed on it before soldering.

When measuring chenier in order to set a cabochon stone in it, ideally the width at the base of the stone should come half way across the wall thickness of the chenier. A seat is then cut out for the stone to sit on, in the wall of the chenier, using a bullstick.

A suitably shaped frazier can also be used to make the seat. If the chenier is a little big for the stone, it is possible to solder, or simply place, a piece of wire, the same thickness as the inside of the tube but a little

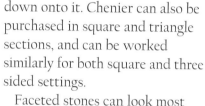

Cabochon sapphires set in chenier.

shorter, into the chenier for the stone to sit on. The outside will have to be filed a little to ease pushing it over onto the stone.

If a cabochon stone is gypsy set, a piece of chenier can be soldered into the hole made in the ring, as a seat for the stone. It should have a tight fit and come just below the surface of the top of the ring to leave enough space for the metal to be pushed down onto it. Chenier can also be purchased in square and triangle sections, and can be worked similarly for both square and three sided settings.

Faceted stones can look most attractive set in chenier. The straight-sidedness being somewhat unusual although this naturally does not allow for much light to be reflected.

When setting irregular and uncut stones any of these principles of making settings can apply. Generally, a bezel of some sort is needed. Whether it holds the stone in a continuous strip depends on the shape of the stone, but as long as there is enough metal to hold the stone firmly, anything goes. If wire is used as a claw, it should be filed carefully to fit exactly over the stone.

Ring by Deborah Ham.

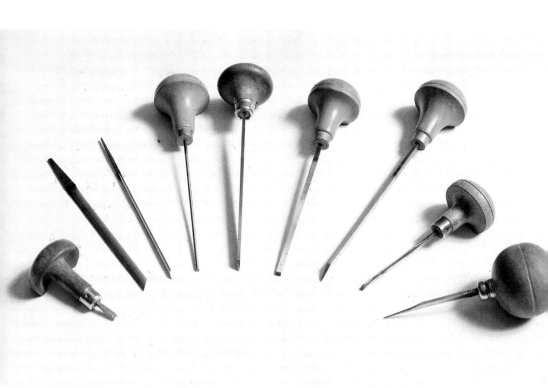

A selection of setting tools.

CHAPTER 3

Settings

This section of the book explains how stones are set. As with most subjects concerned with jewellery making, the more you delve into it the more involved it becomes. I confess to not being a stone setter. I feel more than happy to set my own cabochons and some of the simpler faceted stones. But, like most of my colleagues, having prepared the ring up to the moment of setting I prefer to pack up and send the more precious or fragile stones to the master setter Tony Tigg, whose hands are photographed in this section, who works miracles in a few hours, to complete the picture. That having been said, knowing the theory behind some of the more complicated settings is always useful. Understanding what actually happens to the metal and how it is manipulated to hold the stone is fascinating. It also helps the setter if you know exactly where and how the stone is to be set. But it also takes a lifetime of only setting stones to be as able and agile as Tony.

Jeweller's wax

Jeweller's or setter's wax can be used to hold small items firm whilst working on them. It comes in a solid block. For holding small items such as rings and collets, the wax can be melted into a piece of copper tubing 22mm diameter x 100mm long, with a plate soldered across the bottom. The tubing can then be held in a hand vice and the copper pipe gently heated up to soften the wax which allows the item either to be placed in it or removed from it. A ring holder was used in all the following settings.

RUB OVER SETTINGS

SETTING 1 (a)
Related to ring 2 and mount 1

Rub over setting on cabochon garnet.

1. The ring is held firmly in a 'ring holder'. Keeping the ring holder firm is easier if it can be supported in a wooden pin with a curve, in the front.

The stone should sit comfortably inside the bezel. There should be no large gaps between the stone and the bezel. If the stone does not quite fit, the inside of the bezel can be thinned by removing some of the metal with a 'bullstick' or an abrasive tool in the pendant motor. Keep offering up the stone until it fits.

TIP *I always keep a little piece of blue tack handy, to pick up the stone. It is much easier to hold when trying it in the setting and, you are less likely to drop the stone when holding it with blue tack.*

The pusher
Most rub over settings are done with

a 'pusher'. This is a little tool made from brass, with a wooden handle that sits comfortably in the palm of your hand. The brass end is flat, but the edges are sloped away from the flat face, so that they do not mark the metal that is being pushed over. It should be kept clean and shiny.

2. The pusher is held against one side of the bezel and pushed over and towards the stone. This action is then repeated on the opposite side. The same action is repeated on the two other opposite sides. This should just hold the stone in place so that the whole bezel can be pushed over. Keep working from opposite sides.

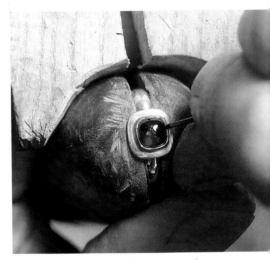

3. Once the bezel is sitting neatly round the stone, the top is pushed down flat next to the stone to close any small gaps.

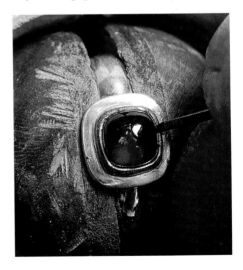

4. Any marks on the outside edges are then cleaned with a file.

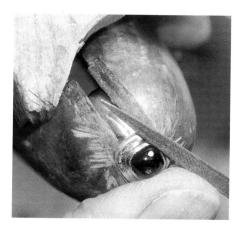

5. A burnisher is used to polish up the outside edge of the bezel.

6. The top edge is then neatened by running round it with a half round 'spitstick'. If you do not have one of these, a fine flat needle file can be used, but take great care that the file does not touch the stone and mark it.

SETTING 1 (b) Related to ring 6a
Rub over on cabochon sapphire

1. On the hollow ring, on page 31, I wanted to give a wide edge to the setting. The top was filed down first so that the stone would sit in at the correct level and then the top edge was pushed down, with the pusher, onto the stone.

It was cleaned up using a burnisher around the top edge.

SETTING 1(c)

Rub over on cabochon tourmaline

The mount on page 83 was used for this cabochon tourmaline. It was made like this to allow the light in from behind the stone.

2. A seat was cut with a 'bullstick' for the stone to sit on.

The stone was set by pushing from opposite sides to fix it and then

filing a little from the corners until they pushed easily over onto the stone. The whole edge was gently pushed over and then flattened with a U tool and burnished.

SETTING 1 (d)
Chenier rub over setting for black onyx bullet

The chenier was soldered in to the anticlastic ring described on page 47. A seat is cut for the stone to sit on, either with a bullstick, or by using a frazier in the pendant motor. Basically, a bullet stone is just a high-sided cabochon. You just have to make sure that the bezel comes

high enough up the stone to hold it in firmly.

The pusher is used to press the sides of the chenier up against the stone and then to push down around the top.

1. This is then cleaned with a file and burnished.

SETTING 1 (e)

To set this large labradorite stone I used the D section wire surround shown on page 74, mount 3. The main ring was held in a ring holder which I fastened into a peg vice which is fixed mounted onto a large floor standing wooden block, so that I had good access all the way round. This saves having to keep taking the holder out of the vice to turn the ring round as the stone is being set.

Using a little flat punch and small jeweller's hammer, I tapped the top of the silver surround so that it folded down onto the stone just enough to hold it in place. It takes quite a long time to really get the D

section sitting where you want it, so don't give up! The silver will need to be cleaned up with a needle file and wet and dry papers afterwards, taking care not to scratch the stone with either.

SETTING 2
Claw

This setting relates to the ring mount 5, on page 77.

The ring is held in a ring holder and the edges of the setting are neatened with a triangular needle file.

1. The inside tips of the claws have to be removed to create a ledge for the girdle of the stone to sit on. This also allows the claw to be pushed easily down onto the stone. About half the thickness of metal is removed to half way down each claw, with a 'chisel' cutter.

The stone is offered up, to gauge whether the claws need spreading a

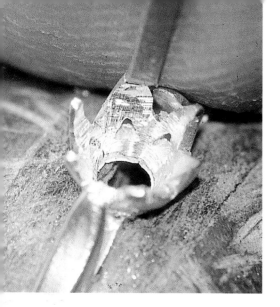

little or if they should be pushed in a little, for a good fit.

2. The tips of the claws are now straightened by holding them with a pair of pliers and carefully bending them up.

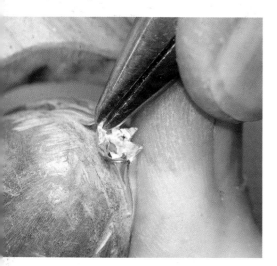

The outside tips of each claw are neatly filed before the stone is placed into the setting. The stone is turned in the setting to check for the best position.

3. A small pusher is used to push the claws down over onto the stone.
If the claws are tough to push down, file the tips a little more, until they push over more easily.

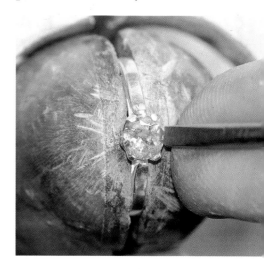

4. File the top edges of the claws to a neat V.

The claws can then be burnished down onto the stone and polished with a buff stick.

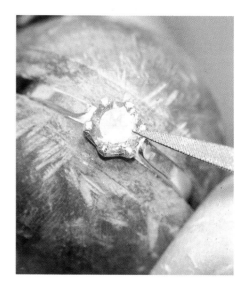

94

SETTING 3
Gypsy Setting (relates to ring 8(a))
For an oval faceted sapphire.

1. After the initial hole has been drilled, it is opened out and shaped with a bullstick. Great care is taken to ensure that the very top of the opening remains a close fit to the top of the stone, as it is this little bit which is pushed down later to hold the stone in.

The cutting of the hole should follow the lines of the stone as closely as possible. This will allow the stone to sit straight and not wobble when it is being set.

3. A pusher is then used to push the metal down around the top of stone.

2. As the stone is placed into the hole, the girdle should sit just below the surface.

4. When the metal is all pushed onto the stone, the edge line is cleaned up with the half-round scorper.
The setting can then be polished with a burnisher and a buff stick.

SETTING 4

*A faceted flourite in a rectangular setting
(relates to ring 4)*
The mount described on page 81 is
soldered to the ring.

the corners are flattened a little to
follow the corners of the stone.

1. The inside edges of the collet are
opened out with a bullstick as
necessary for the stone to fit.

3. The corners are raised to a more
vertical position with pliers so that
it is not so far to push them over
with the pusher. The stone is placed
into the setting and, starting with
one corner the pusher is used to
push the metal over, continuing the
pushing from opposite corners.

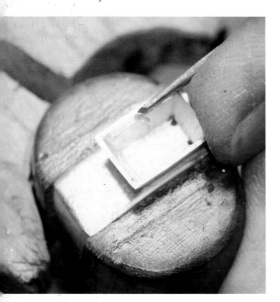

2. The outside edges are filed to
make them easier to push over, and

4. The metal is then pushed down round all the edges onto the stone. Any areas that are difficult to move can be filed a little more to help the pushing.

5. The top edge of the metal is then neatened with a file and polished up with a burnisher.

SETTING 5
Tension set faceted tourmaline (relates to ring 7)

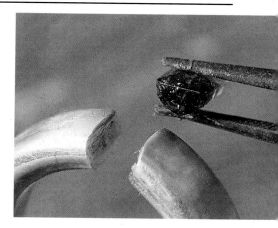

A spitstick sharpened on one side is used to raise the grain which holds in the stone.

1. When the profile of the stone has been filed into the ends of the metal, offer up the stone for fitting.
The ring will have to be opened up a fraction for the stone to slide into position. This can be done between the fingers or by sliding the ring onto a mandrel until it has opened sufficiently to slide the stone into it.

Once the stone is in position, it is held at either end with grains raised from the metal close to its base.

SETTING 6

Outside claw setting for oval semi-faceted tourmaline (relating to mount 6)

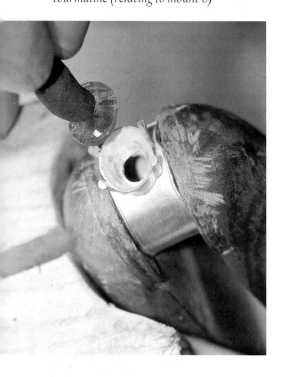

1. Check to make sure that the girdle of the stone is sitting on the top of the bezel.

2. The inside of the D section claw is filed a little, away from the top edge. This allows for easier bending over the stone.

3. The ends of the claws are rounded with a needle file. The claws are then held in the pliers and straightened up to make them easier to bend over.

4. The claws are bent down onto the stone with the pusher.

The setting is polished and finished with a burnisher.

SETTING 7

Pave setting for two faceted rubies and a diamond in a plain gold ring.

There are different types of pave settings, which can be used decoratively as well as for practical reasons. The fancy work that can be shown between the stones becomes as integral to the design of the whole piece as the stones themselves.

Having watched Tony as closely as I could without being set into the ring myself, the skill required to push, cajole and command the metal to do what is required is extraordinary and requires a very practised hand. For those students wishing to become stone setters, don't be discouraged. As we are all well aware, practise makes perfect, and good pave settings need plenty of that!

The ring here is a plain 9 carat gold band, made from 4mm square wire. I wanted two rubies and one diamond set in a line. Each stone was 2.4mm diameter.

I marked the position for the holes at 4mm from centre to centre. I then drilled a 1 mm hole through the ring on each marked dot.

1. At this stage the ring is ready to send to the setter. The holes can be opened out a little with a small frazier on the pendant motor or with a dim stick, but I prefer the setter to do this.

2. The setter then ensures that the stones fit comfortably into their designated holes.

3. A spitstick is then used to dig into the metal at four opposite sides of each stone. This action causes a slight bump to occur in the side of the hole, which helps to grip the stone and also raises a slice of the metal over the stone which holds it in.
The area in between the stones which quite clearly shows as the flat piece in this photo, is then cut so that it matches the grains which hold the stones in place.

4. This is achieved by cutting away a diamond shape to leave just a little raised area in the centre.

5. A line is then cut, to define the outline of the setting and which clears the areas below, above and to the side of the stones.
All the grains are then rounded with a 'graining' tool, shown here with the finished setting.

SETTING 8

Setting cabochon sapphires into a multiple chenier setting (relates to Ring 5b)

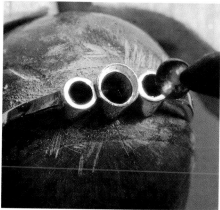

possible to push over the setting all the way round the stone. This is compensated for, by making an undercut in the area next to the

1. A seat is cut, using a bullstick, in each end of the chenier for the stone to sit on. The middle stone is set first as there is no interference from the other two settings. It is a straightforward rub over setting onto the stone.

2. As the other two settings are soldered to the first, it is not

central chenier, which allows the stone to tuck under it, as it is placed onto its seat for setting.

SETTING 9

Setting a faceted tourmaline from behind
(relates to Mount 4)

1. The stone is offered up into the setting to check the correct fit.

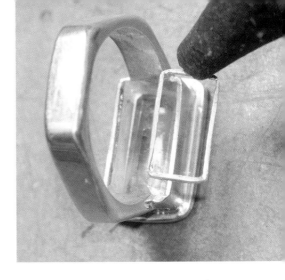

3. The wire surround is placed into the back of the ring with a pair of tweezers or (held with blue tack) and pushed down into the area between the stone and its surround.

4. Grains are raised up against the wire surround to hold it in, using a bullstick.

2. Make sure the front is checked to ensure that the stone sits closely into the setting.

A selection of finishing tools

CHAPTER 4

Finishing

Finishing can make or break a piece of jewellery. Whether you choose a matt finish or highly polished result, the process leading up to the end result should always be thorough and each stage completed before the next is begun.

Firescale

This can cause problems in silver which can result in a patchy finish. It does have to be dealt with at some time during either the construction or the finishing of the ring. Luckily the problem does not occur in high carat golds, but it can be found in 9 carat gold. Fine silver of course does not contain the copper, which is the cause of the fire stain problem, but as this is generally too soft to be of practical use for ring making, using it in place of standard silver is rarely the answer.

Firescale can be prevented, if, right at the start of a piece of work, the surface area is painted with either 'Argotec' or simply a coat of borax. The trouble is that this has to be repeated each time the piece is pickled after annealing or soldering, which can be very tedious. However, this can be worthwhile, especially if there are areas which are difficult to clean after everything is soldered together. The important thing to remember when using either of these two anti-oxidants, is that it should not spread into the area that is fluxed ready for soldering. If it does, the solder will be tempted to flow in that direction, rather than into the join.

Firescale can be hidden, by continual pickling in either a warm sulphuric acid pickle, or warm alum, or indeed safety pickle. You will notice that after each immersion, silver will appear to become 'whiter'. This is because a thin layer of fine silver is gradually building up on the surface, which does not oxidise. Unfortunately, unless this layer is built up to be fairly thick, it is more than likely to disappear when filing, cleaning with wet and dry papers, or polishing. If you can arrange for that white layer to be the finished layer, then the firescale will effectively be hidden.

Lastly, it can be removed in the final stages. As it starts to show as a brownish mark during polishing, you can continue to polish until it has disappeared. Be really careful if you do this. It is very easy to loose well defined edges and corners by over polishing.

A little stone, known as a water of Ayr stone is pretty much the best answer to the problem. The dark patches which show after normal polishing are rubbed with the wet stone which makes a sort of paste over the offending area. It is rubbed until the grey firestained area has disappeared. This may take a little time, but it does eventually go! The stone hardly makes any scratches in the silver, so after the firescale has been removed there is very little extra polishing to do.

FILING

At some stage during construction, a ring will need filing. The files used are important, as the wrong file in the wrong place can cause all sorts of nasty lines and scratches. Generally then:

A *Flat file* is used against a flat surface. Even if that surface is curved (as in a ring) the flat side of the file is in contact with a flat area of the metal.

A *curved file*, which is generally shaped as 'Half round' or 'Oval' is used on the inside of a curve, as for example, inside a ring. This file would also be used on the inside of a

bezel or when opening out a round or oval hole.

A *triangular file* is used to make Vs and also in small areas where a flat file cannot go, and where the sloping angle of the side avoids touching a piece of metal which does not need filing. It is also used to file grooves, prior to bending them up.

A *square file* is used to square up a corner or to help open out a hole.

When a considerable amount of metal has to be removed, a large file is used, but as you will have seen, mostly the use in this book is for needle files. They are used until the metal has an overall uniformity and smoothness.

The scratches made by the file will need removing with a series of different wet and dry papers. As their name suggests, you can use them either wet or dry. I tend to use them dry for most work and then wet, for rubbing down enamels. The order to use them in is from the lower 100s upwards, i.e., starting with 240 and going through 400, 600, 800, 1000, to 1200. I usually use just three of them in the correct order to get a good finish.

There are also papers which give a shine to the metal without being abrasive. These are called crocus and flour paper and are used last.

After using wet and dry papers and getting a smooth finish on the metal, the piece is ready to be polished.

POLISHING with a MOTOR

When polishing on a fast revolving mop, the work must be held firmly in both hands. If you think of the mop which is towards you, as a clock, the top of it is at 12 o'clock, the bottom is at 6 o'clock and the bit which is directly opposite you is at 3 o'clock.

You should only use the mop between 4 and 5 o'clock. If the work is held higher or lower than this, it has a strong tendency to be whipped out of your hands with predictably sad results. The work should be held in a direct line with the face of the mop and the edges can be used to polish sides and more awkward places.

There are different grades of polish, used at different stages of polishing metal. Usually, the polishing is done in this order.

Tripoli	A brown polish, leaves a rather dull finish, but is a good polish for removing scratches.
Hyfin	A white intermediate polish. It gives a hard bright finish.
Green	A good all purpose polish/can be followed by 'rouge'.
Rouge	The polish for a high shine. It is quite messy and can be dipped in methylated spirit to make it less dusty. Or on its own.

A different mop is used for each polish. One polish should not be allowed to stray onto another one's mop!

Matt finishes

These can be achieved in several ways. I usually polish first and then take the surface back to the matt. A matt surface will not hide little blemishes, in fact they tend to show more in a matt surface than a polished one.

Steel Mop — This fits onto the spindle of the polishing motor and is a series of steel threads which hit the surface of the metal in a light way to give a satiny finish.

Glassbrush — This brush is made from glass fibre strands, so should be used under running water. Little pieces can find their way under the skin, so it is preferable to wear rubber gloves. However, it does give a lovely matt look to the metal.

Brassbrush — A brassbrush is always used with a liquid soap, as without it, a rather grey metallic look is left on the surface. Brass brushes can be attached to the polishing motor, the pendant motor, or you can use a hand held one.

Pummice — Pummice powder is an abrasive grey powder which will give an excellent matt appearance, if somewhat dull. It is mixed to a paste with water and applied with an old toothbrush or similar.

Burnisher — A burnisher is a polished tool made from hard steel. They can be straight or curved and will shine any surface when they are rubbed firmly against it.

Steel wool — Different grades of fine steel wool can be used with liquid soap very successfully for a matt finish.

Carbon — Can be used with oil to rub on a polished surface to make it matt.

SIZING

The method of measuring the length needed for a ring is described in the first section. Here we will look at altering the size of a ring once it has been made.

There are two stages when the size can be altered. The first is before a stone has been set and the second is after that. It is definitely better to try to size it at the first stage!

TO SIZE DOWN

Assess the actual size of the ring on a ring stick or mandrel and make a binding wire ring (as in Ring 1, see page 14) on the exact spot. Cut through it and spread it out. Make another binding wire ring around the size that you need, cut through it and spread it out. The difference between the two lengths is the amount you need to remove from the actual ring. Set your dividers to that measurement. Cut through the ring on the solder join and place the dividers against the side of the cut you wish to remove and draw a line. Cut through that line and bend the two ends, so that they sit close together again, and solder them up. The ring can be re-shaped on the mandrel.

TO SIZE UP

Assess how much extra needs to be put in the ring in the same way as sizing down. Although in this case, the difference in the lengths of the binding wire is the amount you need to add rather than subtract. You will need a piece of metal with the same proportions as the ring. It is perfectly OK to add a piece which is bigger all round, as it can be filed away once it is soldered. But do not use a piece which is, for example, thinner than the ring shank, as you will not be able to disguise the difference. Cut through the ring on the solder line and line up one side at a time with the insert, to be soldered. It is much easier to get a good fit if you solder one end at a time. The insert|is then filed and polished to match the rest of the ring.

Most stones cannot withstand any direct heat. Even hard stones, like diamonds, may change their colour when heated, although generally they will stand up well in the heat. Some stones are simply too soft to worth risking and have to be removed before attempting any heating. One way to work on the bottom of a shank without harming the stone, is to hang it upside down, with the top stone immersed in cold water, and use a hot flame to solder a new join in the exposed end of the shank.

A Micro welder is also a useful tool for this sort of hot direct heat, and you may find one in a well-equipped workshop.

UNSETTING A STONE

Use a thin flat-headed tool, where the tip just fits down the side of the stone. There are fine dental tools which will do this, as well as somthing like a blunt blades from a craft knife. Once a little area has been raised away from the stone, it is not difficult to wiggle the tool carefully around the rest of the bezel to remove the stone. Take care not to mark the edge of the stone. After the ring has been sized, the stone is re-set and the bezel cleaned up again.

Peter Page

Gallery

Chris Carpenter

Note: Particular thanks to Jöel Degen who took many of the photographs in the Gallery

Alan Vallis

James Barker

Andrea Berkey

Barbara Christie

Barbara Christie

Andrea Berkey

Chris Carpenter

Alex Goodman

Nick Aikman

Jinks McGrath

Chris Carpenter

Lori Talcott

Mark Nuell

Elke Storch

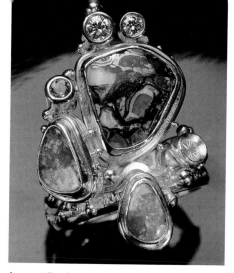

James Barker

Mark Nuell

Jo Swan

Tom Herman

Daphne Krinos

Daphne Krinos

Stefan Friedmann-Cardillac

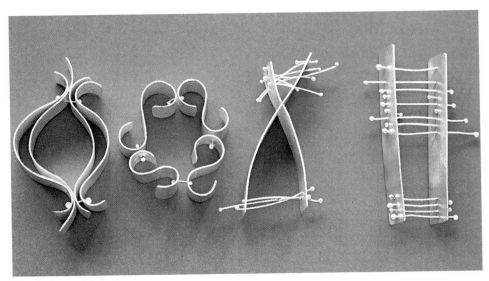

Laura Lapachin

Shelby Fitzpatrick

Lilian Busch

Mikala Djorup

Angie Watts

Elizabeth Olver

Deborah Daher

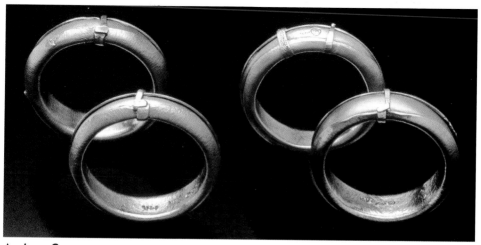

Andrew Cooperman

Anna Chan

Jean Scott-Moncrieff

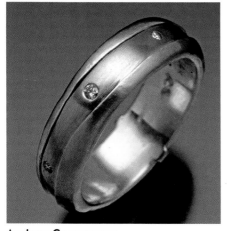

Andrew Cooperman

Elizabeth Olver

Andrea Jones

Anna Chan

Julia Keyte

Kalansbey

Janice Derrick

119

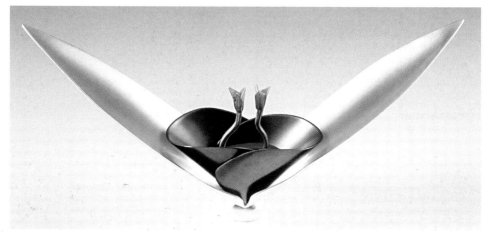

Sue Amendolara

Jinks McGrath

Sarah King

Adam Paxon

Sarah Hood

120

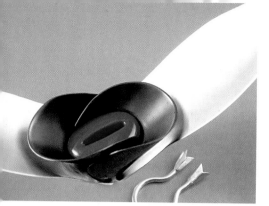

Sue Amendolara

Alison Baxter

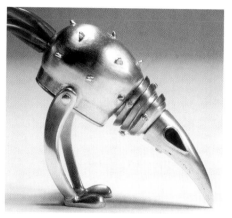

Ri Taniguchi

Nicole Jacquard

Sarah Hood

121

Glossary

Anneal – Applying heat to a metal which allows it to become soft enough to work easily.

Argotec – a white powder painted on silver before heating which helps prevent fire stain.

Ball pein hammer – standard hammer with one rounded end and one flat end.

Barrel polisher – electric motor with rubber drum filled with stainless steel shot, water and polishing medium which burnishes and cleans silver and gold.

Bearer wire – ledge inside a collet or bezel for the base of the stone to sit on.

Bezel – collar round the stone which is bent over to hold it in.

Binding wire – metal wire used to hold pieces together when soldering. Should never be immersed in pickling solution.

Borax/flux – medium applied to metal before soldering to prevent oxidisation thus allowing the solder to run.

Buff stick – wooden stick with leather end, used in hand polishing.

Bullstick – small engraving tool with handle, used to enlarge the inside of a setting.

Burnisher – small stainless steel tool which when rubbed firmly against the metal will produce a shine.

Cabochon – refers to the cut of a stone, i.e. stone cut with smooth curved top and flat bottom.

Carborundum stone – stone used to rub down enamels. Can be course, medium or fine.

Casting – way of producing rings, etc. by forcing molten metal into a cavity left by melting wax, etc.

Chenier – silver and gold tubing.

Collet – strip of metal shaped to fit round the outside of a stone so that it can be set.

Coping saw – medium sized hand saw used for cutting wood and some waxes.

Crocus paper – fine polishing paper used dry.

Culet – the bottom point of a faceted stone.

Cuttlefish – backbone of fish suitable for simple casting.

Dividers – drawing instrument with two adjustable points. Invaluable for all precise measurements and drawings.

Faceted – cut of stone. Facets are flattened sides made on stones to reflect the light to their full advantage.

Flat nosed pliers – pliers where both inside edges are flat.

Flux enamel – colourless enamel used as an undercoat mainly on silver to prevent fire stain.

Forging – method of shaping and curving metal using hammer and shaped metal stakes.

Former – metal or wooden shape used to bend and shape the metal around.

Fusing – joining metal together by heating close to melting temperature. No solder is used when fusing.

Glassbrush – brush used to clean and degrease metal made from glass fibres.

Gypsey Set – stone setting where the stone appears to sit in the metal without any visible means of being held in.

Half round pliers – pliers with one flat and one curved inside edge.

Jewellers/setter's wax – wax used to hold a finished article while setting a stone or other into it.

Mandrel – tapered steel tool used for shaping rings, bracelets, necklaces, etc.

Needle file – small hand files with variety of profiles, i.e. flat, oval, round, half round, triangular, square, etc.

Paillon – small piece of solder.

Pendant motor – electric handheld tool to which a variety of heads can be fitted. Used for drilling, polishing, texturing, etc.

Pickle – medium used to clean metal after heating, annealing and soldering.

Planishing hammer – hammer used to smooth out marks made previously by other hammers. The face of which is kept highly polished.

Pummice powder – grey abrasive powder moistened to make a paste applied with a brush or finger to clean metal.

Pusher – small hand tool used to push edge of collet or bezel over onto the stone.

Quench – having been heated or soldered an article is quenched in cold water before being cleaned in pickle.

Ring Holder – handheld wooden vice type tool which holds a ring whilst stone is being set into it.

Rolling mill – tool used to reduce thickness of metal sheet and shape of metal wire under pressure.

Scriber – steel tool with sharp point used to mark fine lines on on metal.

Shank – the shape of the metal that goes round the finger that holds the mount.

Sinusoidal stake – curved and tapered metal stake.

Solder – alloy of metal to be joined that melts at a lower temperature than the metal.

Titanium soldering stick – titanium stick with handle used to alter and move items during soldering process.

Wet and dry paper – abrasive papers from coarse to fine used either with water or dry to clean metal.

Suppliers

UK

Ballou Findings
15 Cochran Close
Crowhill
Milton Keynes
MK8 0AJ
Tel: 01908 569 311
Fax: 01908 260 262
(Findings)

Michael Bloomstein
30 Gloucester Road
Brighton
BN1 4AQ
Tel: 01273 608374
(Metals)

J. Blundell & Son
199 Wardour Street
London
W1V 4JN
Tel: 020 7437 4746
(Metals)

Cookson's Precious Metals Ltd
49 Hatton Garden
London
EC1N 8YS
Tel: 020 7400 6500
Fax: 020 7400 6511
(Metals)

Holts
Hatton Garden
London
EC1N 8YS
Tel: 020 7405 5286
(Stone dealers)

Prabhu Enterprises Ltd
Suite D
32-34 Greville Street
London EC1N 8TB
Tel: 020 7242 4650
(Stone dealers)

Sutton Tools Ltd
37 Frederick Street
Birmingham
B1 3HN
Tel: 0121 236 7139
(Tools)

Virum Signum
9A North Street
Clapham Old Town
London
SW4 0HN
Tel: 020 7627 0840
(Enamels)

H.S. Walsh & Son
21 St Cross Street
Hatton Garden
London
EC1N 8UN
Tel: 020 7242 3711
(Tools)

USA

Allcraft Tool & Supply
666 Pacific Street
Brooklyn
NY 11217
Tel: +718 789 2800
(Tools, kilns)

Anchor Tool & Supply
P.O. Box 265

Chatham
NJ 07928
Tel: +201 635 2094
(Tools and general supplies)

Fire & Borel
119 Third Street
Oakland
CA 94607
Tel: +415 832 0355
Fax: +415 834 6217
(Tools)

Gesswein
255 Hancock Avenue
Bridgeport
CT 06605
Tel: +203 366 5400
Fax: +203 366 3953
(Tools)

T.B Hagstoz & Son
709 Sansom Street
Philadelphia
PA 19106
Tel: +215 922 1627
(Metals and tools)

Hoover & Strong
10700 Trade Road
Richmond
VA 23236
Tel: +804 794 3700
Fax: + 804 794 5687
(Metals)

Rio Grande
7500 Bluewater Road
NW Alburquerque
NM 87121–1962
(Stone dealers and tools)

Myron Toback
25 West 47th Street
New York
NY 10036
Tel: +212 398 8300
Fax: +212 869 0808
(Tools)

Bibliography

Codina, Carles, *Handbook of Jewellery Techniques*, A& C Black Publishers Ltd, 2000

Fisch, Arline M. *Textile Techniques on Metal*, Robert Hale, 1997

McCreight, Tim, *Boxes and Lockets – Metalsmithing Techniques*, A&C Black Publishers Ltd, 1999

McCreight, Tim, *Jewellery – Fundamentals of Metalsmithing*, A&C Black Publishers Ltd, 1998

McGrath, Jinks, *The Encyclopedia of Jewellery Making Techniques*, Headline, 1997

McGrath, Jinks, *First Steps in Enamelling*, Apple Press, 1994

Untracht, Oppi, *Jewellery Concepts and Design*, N.A.G. Press, 1996

Index